やさしい英語を聴いて読む
IBCオーディオブックス

LEVEL
5

レ・ミゼラブル
Les Misérables

ヴィクトル・ユーゴー 原著

ニーナ・ウェグナー リライト

松澤喜好 監修

JN086548

IBCパブリッシング

《使用語彙について》

レベル1：中学校で学習する単語約 1000 語

レベル2：レベル1の単語＋使用頻度の高い単語約 300 語

レベル3：レベル1の単語＋使用頻度の高い単語約 600 語

レベル4：レベル1の単語＋使用頻度の高い単語約 1000 語

レベル5：語彙制限なし

カバーデザイン

岩目地英樹（コムデザイン）

ブックデザイン

鈴木一誌＋藤田美咲

ナレーション

Greg Dale

はじめに

英語の習得をめざす人が夢見るのは、「英語で感動することができる」レベルだと思います。「映画を字幕なしで見て感動したい」「海外ドラマを英語で楽しめるようになりたい」、そんな希望をお持ちのことでしょう。英語で感動し、そして他人をも感動させることができるようになれば、日本語と英語の両方で、人生を2倍楽しむことができてしまうのです。

英語が得意な日本人が最後まで苦しむのが、「リスニング100％」のレベルに到達することです。「リスニング100％」の状態とは、発音、語彙、文法、多読、多聴などで蓄積されたスキルが頭のなかで統合されている状態です。したがって、「リスニング100％」になることを目標にすえて学習することが英語マスターへの近道だと考えられます。しかし現状では、日本人がまとめて長時間の英語の音声を聴く機会は極端に少ないといえます。それに、ただ英語を1日中聴き流していれば目標に到達できるというわけでもありません。自分にあった教材を使用して、自分のレベルを上げていくプロセスを組み立ててこそ、「リスニング100％」の状態をものにすることができるのです。

　これまでリスニングや発音の指導をしていて、リスニング学習へのアプローチを誤ったために伸び悩んでいる生徒にたくさん接してきました。彼らはそろってある典型的な誤りに陥っていたのです。これは最初に目標として定めたレベルに達するよりも早く、次の題材へと移ってしまうことに起因します。これではレベルアップの機会を自らつぶしていることになります。もっと分かりやすく説明しましょう。

● Question
　ここに1冊の日常英会話の練習用CDがあったとします。このCDの再生時間は60分間で、20章で構成されているとしましょう。あなたなら、このCDを使ってどのように練習しますか。以下の3とおりの方法を見てみましょう。

例1 　1章ずつ順番に1回ずつ声に出して発音しながら練習する。ひととおり終わったら、もう一度最初から20章を通して練習する。

……この方法では、一応1冊を終わらせてはいますが、発音やリスニングの練習としては、まったく不十分です。ではもう少し量を増やせばよいのでしょうか。

例2 　1章を5回くりかえしてから次の章に移る。20章まで同様にして、練習する。

……いわゆる勉強家のやりかたで、ご立派だと思います。この方法にはそれなりの勉強時間を確保する意志が必要だからです。その結果として少しは実力がつくと思われますが、発音やリスニングの練習方法としては、まだまだ不十分でレベルアップにはつながりません。

例3 ひととおり20章を最後まで聴いてから、一番好きな章をひとつだけ選ぶ。その章を携帯オーディオ機器にダウンロードして常に持ち歩き、50回から100回くりかえす。

……この方法なら、カタカナ式だった英語が、ようやく本来の英語に変身します。20章のうちのたったひとつの章をくりかえし聴けばよいので、例2と総合的な所要時間は一緒ですが、心理的な負担がぐっと軽くなります。

　なぜ例3の方法がもっとも有効なのかを、スポーツにたとえて説明しましょう。テニスでも野球でも、ラケットやバットの素振りをおこないます。素振りは、5回や10回では身につきません。数千回くりかえすことで、筋肉がつき、敏しょう性が備わり、やがて球を確実に返せるようになります。同様に、発音やリスニングも、カタカナ式発音から英語本来の発音へと変身するために必要な顔の筋肉、呼吸方法、確実性、敏しょう性を身につけるためには、数百回の練習が必要なのです。例2では、素振りの筋肉がつく前に次の練習に入ってしまっています。それに対して例3の方法なら、短い題材を何度もくりかえすことで、短時間のうちに急速に力がつくのです。

●オウムの法則

　ここまでで述べてきたことはParrot's Law「オウムの法則」に基づいています。これは私がオウムの調教にちなんで名づけた考えかたです。オウムは2,000回くりかえして初めてひとつの言葉を口にできるようになるといいます。たとえばまず「おはよう」ならそれを2,000回くりかえし教えます。ついに「おはよう」と言わせることに成功すれば、次にはたった200回の訓練で「こんばんは」が言えるようになります。英語学習もこれと同じで、早い段階で脳に英語の発音を刷

り込んでおくことが重要なのです。Parrot's Lawのねらいはそこにあります。日本人の英語学習法を見てみると、「おはよう」をマスターする前に「こんばんは」の練習に取りかかってしまうので、いつまでたってもひとことも話せないし、聴こえない状態に留まってしまうのです。オウムですら一生に一度、2,000回のくりかえしをするだけで言葉を発することを覚えます。鳥よりもはるかに学習能力が高い人間なら、100回もくりかえせば、カタカナ式発音をほんものの英語発音に変身させることができるはずです。

● 短い英文を１００回聴く

発音やリスニングが苦手な方は、まず短めの題材をひたすらくりかえし聴いて、英語の発音を完全に習得してしまいましょう。Parrot's Lawのメソッドなら、短い題材から大きな効果が期待できます。最初の50回までは、毎回少しずつ発見があり、自分の成長が実感できます。さすがに50回を超えると発音方法が分かるようになり、意味もほぼ理解して、英語で直接、場面をイメージできるようになります。同時に、自分の進歩が飽和してきて「これ以上は伸びないのでは？」と感じられます。でも実際には、50回を超えてからが肝心なのです。100回に向けて、脳に音の刷り込みをおこなっていきます。子音、母音、音節、イントネーション、複数の単語のかたまり、間の取りかた、息継ぎまでをそっくり再現できるまで練習しましょう。こうしてオウムでいうところの「おはよう」レベルに達することができるのです。

● 仕上げの３０分間

次にもう少し長めの20分から30分くらいの題材を聴いて、ストーリーを追ってみます。そしてそれを数十回くりかえし聴きます。これ

がParrot's Lawメソッドの仕上げ段階です。これにより、リスニングレベルは劇的に向上します。まったく未知のストーリーでも、英語で筋を追うことができるようになるのです。

　一生のうち一度、短い英文の朗読を100回くりかえして聴き、練習するだけで、発音とリスニングの壁を越えることができるのです。英語学習の早い時期に絶対に実施すべきトレーニングだと考えています。

●オーディオブックス

　アメリカでは、ベストセラーをオーディオブックスで楽しむスタイルが普及しています。ストーリーを味わいながら英語のリスニングスキルを伸ばしたいなら、オーディオブックスを聴いて想像力を働かせることがとても効果的です。しかしその一方で、ネイティブスピーカーを対象とした一般のオーディオブックスをいきなり聴いて挫折してしまう人がたくさんいることも事実です。日本の読者に向けた『IBCオーディオブックス』なら、楽しみながらParrot's Lawメソッドを実行することができます。『IBCオーディオブックス』のラインナップからお好きなものをチョイスして、挫折することなしにストーリーを楽しんでみてください。

『IBCオーディオブックス』活用法

　前述したようにアメリカでは、ベストセラーをオーディオブックスで楽しむスタイルが一般化しています。ストーリーを楽しみつつ英語のリスニングスキルを伸ばしたい人に、オーディオブックスはとても効果的だといえます。ところが、日本人英語学習者がいきなりネイティブスピーカー用のオーディオブックスを聴いても、スピードや語彙の問題から、挫折感を味わうだけとなってしまうかもしれません。英語初心者でも楽しみながら英語に親しめる『IBCオーディオブックス』は、いままでまとめて長時間の英語の音声に触れる機会がなかった日本の英語学習者に、初級から上級まで、幅広い音声を提供します。語彙のレベルや朗読のスピードが豊富なラインナップからお好みのタイトルを選び、上手に活用していただければ、リスニングをマスターすることが可能になります。

　では具体的に、『IBCオーディオブックス』を120%使いこなす方法を説明しましょう。

1　自分の心のままに「お気に入り」のトラックをみつける

　まず、『IBCオーディオブックス』のCD全体を、「テキストを見ずに」聴いてください。聴きかたは、音楽CDと同じ感覚でけっこうです。たとえば、買ったばかりの音楽CDを聴くときは、ひととおり聴いて、自分はどの曲が好きで、どの曲が嫌い、と心でチェックを入れています。『IBCオーディオブックス』のCDもまず全体を通して聴いてみて、自分の好きな曲＝トラックをみつけてみます。

　聴いてみて内容が半分ぐらい理解できるようでしたら、テキストを見ないままで何度か続け、好きなトラックをみつけてください。ほとんど理解できない場合は、テキストを見ながら聴いて好きなトラックを選んでもかまいませんが、あくまでも基本は、「テキストを見ないで聴く」ことです。

　最初からほとんど聴き取れてしまった方は、次のステップ②へ進んでください。

　お気に入りのトラックをみつけたら、そこを何度もくりかえし聴いて、リスニングと朗読の練習をしましょう。Parrot's Lawのメソッドの第一歩、短いパートを100回くりかえす方法の実践です。くりかえし回数のめやすはだいたい以下のとおりですが、「自分が納得できるまで」を原則とします。100回より多くても少なくてもけっこうです。
　また、気に入ったトラックは携帯オーディオ機器に入れて持ち歩くと、空き時間をみつけてリスニング回数をかせぐことができますので、おすすめです。

- 30回程度、テキストを見ないで、ひたすらリスニングをおこなう。
- 次の30回は、テキストを見ながら、内容を理解する。
- 次の30回は、CDに続いて自分でも声を出して発音する。
- 次の10回で、テキストを見ないでリスニングが100%になった状態を確認する。

　これだけの練習を終えるころには、自分が選んだトラックについては、すべて理解できるようになっていることと思います。時間的には短いですが、練習の最後には、「リスニング100%」の状態を体験してみることが重要です。テキストを見ながら内容を理解している段階においては、積極的に辞書を引いて、発音もチェックしておい

てください。聴くだけでなく自分自身でも発音してみる次のステップに入るころには、文章をほぼ暗記できていると思います。

短めの1トラックを題材にして、じゅうぶんすぎるくらいに練習できたら、いよいよ、1冊全部を聴いてみてください。練習する前とくらべて驚くほど聴き取れるようになっている自分を発見するはずです。

2 リスニングと朗読の練習をする

ステップ①では、短めの1トラックだけに集中しましたが、このステップ②では、20分から30分程度の長めのリスニングをおこないます。ステップ①で選んだトラックを含む、前後20分程度のトラックを連続してくりかえし聴き、あわせて発音練習もします。全部で100回といいたいところですが、20回から30回でもじゅうぶんだと思います。聴きかたと練習法については、下記を参考にしてください。

- 10回程度、テキストを見ないで、ひたすらリスニングをおこなう。
- 次の10回は、テキストを見ながら、内容を理解する。
- 次の10回は、CDに続いて自分でも声を出して発音する。
- 次の5回で、テキストを見ないで、リスニングが100％になった状態を確認する。

3 ストーリーを楽しむ

以上の練習でリスニング力と正しい発音がしっかりと身についてきます。自分でもじゅうぶん練習したと納得できたら、本1冊分、トラック全部を通して聴いてみてください。練習を始める前とは見違えるように聴き取れると思います。リスニングでストーリーを追える自分に気づいて感動すると思います。この感動が、英語の学習を続ける大きなモチベーションになります。

　英語でストーリーを楽しむという経験を味わうことによって、いままでの英語学習方法に変化が起きてきます。たとえば、子音・母音の発音方法についてもっと興味がわいてきて、真の発音練習ができるようになったりします。自身の語彙不足に気づいたり、これまで発音を正確に身につけていなかったことなどに気づくことで、辞書を引いたときにはその単語の発音までもチェックするようになります。いったんストーリーを楽しめるようになると、英語を語順のとおり直接理解していく習慣がつきます。英文をいちいち日本語に直したり、文末から後戻りしないと理解できないという状態が改善されます。洋書を読んでいても文章を単語の発音と結びつけられるようになります。聴くときも、読むときも、バラバラの単語単位ではなくて、複数の単語どうしのかたまりで意味をとらえていけるようになります。

　英会話や、英語でのプレゼンテーションにもよい影響が出始めます。発音の指導をしていると、「発音明快・意味不明」の人に出会います。発音はネイティブスピーカーレベルなのですが、目をつぶって聴いていても意味が伝わってこない人のことです。そうなってしまう最大の原因は、「伝える」ということを明確にイメージせずに、ただ英語を話しているところにあります。そうすると英語のイントネーションや、単語のかたまりごとのスピード調節、間の取りかたなどがないがしろにされてしまい、聴き手に意味が伝わらないのです。たとえネイティブスピーカーでも英単語をぶつ切りにして話をされれば、意味がわからなくなってしまうのです。ところが、リスニングによってストーリーを楽しめる段階までくれば、この「発音明快・意味不明」の状態は自然に改善されていきます。ストーリーを楽しめることは、ネイティブスピーカーの聴こえかたに近づいてくるからです。

4 『IBCオーディオブックス』のさきにあるもの

　自信がついてきたら、さらに『IBCオーディオブックス』からほかのタイトルを選んで楽しんでください。日本人の英語学習者は、そもそも英語に触れる絶対量が不足しているので、もっと積極的に英語に触れる機会をつくる必要があるのです。『IBCオーディオブックス』には難易度に合わせたレベル表示があるので、それを参考に、どんどんレベルの高いストーリーに進んでください。ただし、それを勉強としてとらえてしまってはいけません。楽しみながら実践した結果として大量の英語に触れている、というのが理想的です。英語に触れることを日常の習慣として取り入れることから始めるのです。

　そして、だんだんと実力がついてきたら、好きな映画やペーパーバック、海外のオーディオブックスなども取り入れてみましょう。1日1時間としても、楽しみながら、1週間で7時間もの間、英語に触れていることが可能となります。それだけの時間、英語漬けといえる環境に身を置けば、英語を流しっぱなしにしているだけでも、どんどん実力がアップしていくでしょう。

　皆さんも『IBCオーディオブックス』で、英語を聴くことの楽しみを自分のものにしていってください。

● 本書のテキストは小社より刊行の「ラダーシリーズ」と共通です。

● 「あらすじ」のトラック番号は付属のCDに対応しています。2枚組のときは左がCD、右がトラックの番号となります。

● 本書のCDは、CDプレーヤーでご利用ください。パソコンのCDドライブなどでは正常に再生できない場合があります。

目次

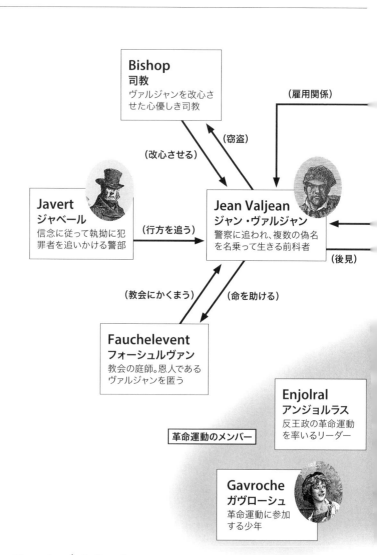

Bishop
司教
ヴァルジャンを改心させた心優しき司教

（雇用関係）

（窃盗）

（改心させる）

Javert
ジャベール
信念に従って執拗に犯罪者を追いかける警部

（行方を追う）

Jean Valjean
ジャン・ヴァルジャン
警察に追われ、複数の偽名を名乗って生きる前科者

（後見）

（教会にかくまう）

（命を助ける）

Fauchelevent
フォーシュルヴァン
教会の庭師。恩人であるヴァルジャンを匿う

Enjolral
アンジョルラス
反王政の革命運動を率いるリーダー

革命運動のメンバー

Gavroche
ガヴローシュ
革命運動に参加する少年

Illustrations: Émile Bayard

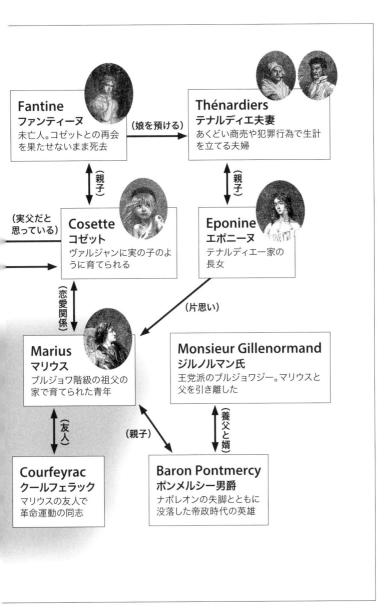

Fantine
ファンティーヌ
未亡人。コゼットとの再会を果たせないまま死去

（娘を預ける）

Thénardiers
テナルディエ夫妻
あくどい商売や犯罪行為で生計を立てる夫婦

（親子）

（実父だと思っている）

Cosette
コゼット
ヴァルジャンに実の子のように育てられる

（親子）

Eponine
エポニーヌ
テナルディエ家の長女

（恋愛関係）

（片思い）

Marius
マリウス
ブルジョワ階級の祖父の家で育てられた青年

Monsieur Gillenormand
ジルノルマン氏
王党派のブルジョワジー。マリウスと父を引き離した

（友人）

（親子）

（養父と婿）

Courfeyrac
クールフェラック
マリウスの友人で革命運動の同志

Baron Pontmercy
ポンメルシー男爵
ナポレオンの失脚とともに没落した帝政時代の英雄

TRACK 1-1 p.30~

Part I: Fantine I　ファンティーヌ（1）

パン1つを盗んだことが元で19年間服役したジャン・ヴァルジャンは、彼に食事とベッドを提供した司教の家で銀の皿を盗む。翌朝ヴァルジャンを取り押さえた警官らが司教の家にくるが、司教は、皿は自分が譲ったものなので彼を解放するようにと言う。（6分03秒）

キーワード

☐ ragged 　　☐ ex-convict 　　☐ bishop 　　☐ desperation
☐ galley 　　☐ astound 　　☐ cunning 　　☐ pang

TRACK 1-2 p.36~

Part I: Fantine II　ファンティーヌ（2）

数年後、ファンティーヌという女性が、夫に先立たれて仕事を探すために、パリ郊外で宿屋を営むテナルディエ一家に娘のコゼットを預ける。テナルディエ家の人たちは、ファンティーヌがいなくなるとコゼットを召使いにように扱った。（1分59秒）

キーワード

☐ suburb 　　☐ widow 　　☐ afford 　　☐ immediate
☐ expense 　　☐ grateful 　　☐ willingness 　　☐ servant

TRACK 1-3 p.39~

Part I: Fantine III　ファンティーヌ（3）

ムッシュ・マドレーヌという男が、モントルイユ＝シュル＝メールの町で大成功を収める。町の人たちが敬愛する中、ジャヴェール警視だけが疑いの目で見ていた。ある日、町である労働者が車輪の下敷きになったのを、マドレーヌは力の限りを尽くして助けた。（2分28秒）

キーワード

☐ clasp 　　☐ mantle 　　☐ inspector 　　☐ suspicious
☐ luis 　　☐ startle 　　☐ shiver 　　☐ strain

TRACK 1-4 p.42~

Part I: Fantine IV　ファンティーヌ（4）

市長になったムッシュ・マドレーヌは、その数年後、ファンティーヌからの頼みごとに応えようとした直前、やってきたジャヴェールからの告白を聞く。翌日、ジャン・ヴァルジャンとされる男の裁判に突然現れたマドレーヌは、自分の正体がジャン・ヴァルジャンだと明かす。（4分28秒）

キーワード

☐ mayor　　☐ confess　　☐ dismiss　　☐ denounce
☐ falter　　☐ composure　☐ ashamed　　☐ testify

TRACK 1-5 p.47~

Part I: Fantine V　ファンティーヌ（5）

病床にいるファンティーヌの市長への依頼は、コゼットを連れ戻してくることだった。依頼を果たせぬまま病院を訪れたジャン・ヴァルジャンの元にジャヴェールが現れる。娘に会うことができない運命を悟ったファンティーヌは失意のまま息を引き取る。（2分47秒）

キーワード

☐ withdrew　☐ saving　　☐ weigh　　☐ strode
☐ gleam　　☐ triumph　　☐ limply　　☐ prayer

TRACK 1-6 p.52~

Part II: Cosette I　コゼット（1）

ジャヴェールに拘束されたジャン・ヴァルジャンはその晩脱獄する。数日後、テナルディエという宿屋の主人のところに40歳前後の紳士が現れる。紳士はコゼットの法定後見人だと言い、数千フランをテナルディエに支払うとコゼットを連れて立ち去った。（1分44秒）

キーワード

☐ await　　☐ bundle　　☐ apparently　☐ mourning
☐ legal　　☐ guardian

TRACK 1-7
p.54~

Part II: Cosette II　コゼット（2）

ジャン・ヴァルジャンとコゼットはしばらくの間幸せに暮らしたが、ジャヴェールが追ってきていた。ある晩、コゼットを散歩に連れ出したヴァルジャンは一刻を争う事態に追い込まれ、コゼットをロープで体に結び付けると、壁をよじ登り暗い庭に降り立った。（3分45秒）

キーワード

- [ ] adore
- [ ] strove
- [ ] beggar
- [ ] imposter
- [ ] crept
- [ ] platoon
- [ ] dart
- [ ] scale

TRACK 1-8
p.58~

Part II: Cosette III　コゼット（3）

庭にいた男は、ヴァルジャンが市長のときに車輪の下敷きになったのを助けたフォーシュルヴァンだった。彼らが逃げ込んだ所は修道院で、そこの庭師だったフォーシュルヴァンは院長に彼らを自分の弟と姪だと紹介、留まることを許された二人は救われた。（2分48秒）

キーワード

- [ ] shudder
- [ ] pity
- [ ] embrace
- [ ] convent
- [ ] shack
- [ ] owe
- [ ] enroll
- [ ] content

TRACK 1-9
p.62~

Part III: Marius I　マリウス（1）

マリウスは、ブルジョワで王政主義者の祖父母と暮らしていた。18歳のある日、父が病気であることを聞かされて父の家に向かったマリウスは、通夜を営んでいた司教から父が遺したという紙切れを渡されて、父がナポレオンの下で男爵だったことを知る。（2分56秒）

キーワード

- [ ] colonel
- [ ] baron
- [ ] unrivaled
- [ ] exile
- [ ] restoration
- [ ] traitor
- [ ] vigil
- [ ] crepe

TRACK 1-10
p.65~

Part III: Marius II マリウス（2）

父の死後数か月たったある日曜日、マリウスが教会のある柱の裏手で祈っていると、男が近づいてきて「息子から引き離された父親が毎週日曜日にこの柱に潜んで息子を見て泣いていた」と言った。それが死んだ父と自分のことだとマリウスは気づく。（2分10秒）

キーワード

☐ kneel　　☐ pillar　　☐ pray　　☐ threaten
☐ disinherit　☐ sacrifice　☐ scar　　☐ exclamation

TRACK 1-11
p.68~

Part III: Marius III マリウス（3）

マリウスは図書館で父やワーテルローの戦いの記録を読み、ブルジョワジーや王政主義から脱皮して革命に目覚める。不信を募らせた祖父がマリウスの部屋で「マリウス・ポンメルシー男爵」と刷られた名刺を発見し、翌日マリウスは祖父の家を後にした。（2分45秒）

キーワード

☐ noble　　☐ pursue　　☐ shed　　☐ royalism
☐ republic　☐ card-maker　☐ curious　☐ fury

TRACK 1-12
p.71~

Part III: Marius IV マリウス（4）

経済的な支援を失ったマリウスは、学校を卒業後、必死で働いていた。ある日、久しぶりに公園で散歩をした彼は、そこでよく見かけた男性が、美しい女性と歩いているのを目にするが、その女性がその男性といつも一緒にいた少女だと気づき衝撃を受ける。（3分37秒）

キーワード

☐ stern　　☐ shabby　　☐ surge　　☐ fray
☐ skinny　　☐ ugly　　☐ stroll　　☐ dumbfounded

TRACK 1-13
p.75~

Part III: Marius V マリウス（5）

マリウスの部屋の隣人はテナルディエといい、彼らの家賃滞納を彼が秘密裏に助けたことがあった。ある日マリウスの部屋に長女エポニーヌが父親からの手紙を持って訪ねてきた。壁の穴に気づいたマリウスは好奇心に勝てず、隣の様子をのぞき込んだ。（2分21秒）

キーワード

☐ oblivious　☐ overhear　☐ evict　☐ meantime
☐ invitation　☐ generous　☐ cruel　☐ ponder

TRACK 1-14
p.78~

Part III: Marius VI マリウス（6）

マリウスがのぞいていると、長女が部屋に帰ってきて「あの方がくるわ！」と叫んだ。父親は「わかった、支度だ！」と言うと火を消し、椅子を壊し、妻に病気の振りをしろと言い、下の娘に窓を割らせた。娘がガラスでけがをしたとき、父は「完璧だ」と言った。（1分30秒）

キーワード

☐ carriage　☐ bleed　☐ bandage

TRACK 1-15
p.80~

Part III: Marius VII マリウス（7）

公園の親子が来たのを見てマリウスは仰天した。テナルディエは男性に窮状を訴え、男性が8時にお金を携えて戻ってくると、テナルディエは正体を現して男性に脅迫を始めた。その瞬間ジャヴェールが警官の一団を伴って現れ、男性は混乱に乗じて姿を消した。（4分11秒）

キーワード

☐ overjoyed　☐ fake　☐ child-stealer　☐ bandit
☐ shift　☐ commotion　☐ neglect　☐ unnoticed

TRACK 2-1
p.86~

Part IV: The Rue Plumet I プリュメ街（1）
翌日マリウスは部屋を引き払い旧友の下に身を寄せた。その後も彼はリュクサンプール公園を歩いたが親子には会えなかった。ある日そこでエポニーヌに出会うと、彼女はマリウスに娘の居場所を知っていると言い、二人は娘の家に向かった。（2分01秒）

キーワード

☐ witness ☐ heartbroken ☐ wretched ☐ mend
☐ reception ☐ darken ☐ philanthropist ☐ fancy

TRACK 2-2
p.89~

Part IV: The Rue Plumet II プリュメ街（2）
コゼットが修道院の教育を終えると、ジャン・ヴァルジャンは新しい隠れ家に引っ越した。ある日、コゼットは自分が美しくなったことに気づき、その頃公園でマリウスに出会った。コゼットの変化に気づいたヴァルジャンは若者に嫉妬して公園の散歩をやめた。（3分03秒）

キーワード

☐ nestle ☐ pose ☐ residence ☐ proper
☐ despise ☐ chat ☐ cheerfulness ☐ downcast

TRACK 2-3
p.93~

Part IV: The Rue Plumet III プリュメ街（3）
コゼットが座っていたベンチに戻ると石が置かれていて、その下には恋文があった。夕方ジャン・ヴァルジャンが出かけたあと、コゼットは庭に出てベンチに腰掛けた。振り返るとあの若者が門の所に立っていた。コゼットは若者を庭に招き入れて話をした。（2分48秒）

キーワード

☐ signature ☐ instinctually ☐ breathlessly ☐ flutter
☐ presence ☐ disturb ☐ sublimely

TRACK 2-4 p.96~

Part IV: The Rue Plumet IV ブリュメ街（4）

二人は一か月半ほどの間、晩に庭で落ち合っていたが、コゼットはマリウスに、イングランドに行くことになったことを伝える。コゼットは彼に一緒に来るように頼むが、マリウスは自分に考えがあると言い、明日の晩9時にまた会おうと言って庭を去った。（1分27秒）

キーワード

☐ shatter   ☐ carve   ☐ usual

TRACK 2-5 p.98~

Part IV: The Rue Plumet V ブリュメ街（5）

ベンチでヴァルジャンは二人の密会に気づくが、直後何者かが投げてよこした紙を見て動揺する。次の晩、祖父から結婚の許しを得られなかったマリウスはコゼットの家に行くが、誰もいない。門の外で、彼に友人たちがバリケードで待っていると言う者がいた。（4分43秒）

キーワード

☐ inquire   ☐ despair   ☐ dignity   ☐ plead
☐ devastate   ☐ consent   ☐ numb   ☐ tentatively

TRACK 2-6 p.103~

Part IV: The Rue Plumet VI ブリュメ街（6）

その間、バリケードでは革命家たちが声を潜めて話していた。通りも、通りを防御するためのバリケードも、暗く静まり返っていた。革命家たちのリーダーであるアンジョルラスはガヴローシュという少年にバリケードから出て様子を見てくるように指示をした。（0分51秒）

キーワード

☐ dim   ☐ headquarters

TRACK 2-7
p.105~

Part IV: The Rue Plumet VII　プリュメ街 (7)

マリウスはバリケードに向かいながら一瞬コゼットのことを思った。次の瞬間兵士たちがやって来た。アンジョルラスは「フランス革命！」と叫び、反対側からは「撃て！」と答えがあった。兵士に襲われたクールフェラックとガヴローシュを助けたのはマリウスだった。(2分50秒)

キーワード

☐ musket　　☐ destiny　　☐ comrade　　☐ pause
☐ cast　　　☐ bullet　　　☐ blast　　　　☐ bayonet

TRACK 2-8
p.108~

Part IV: The Rue Plumet VIII　プリュメ街 (8)

兵士がマリウスを銃で撃ったが、弾は銃口をふさいだ何者かの手を貫通した。マリウスは松明と火薬樽を持って壁の上に立ち、「立ち去らないとバリケードを吹き飛ばす」と叫んだ。恐怖におののいた兵士たちは逃げ出し、バリケードは救われた。(1分48秒)

キーワード

☐ muzzle　　☐ keg　　　　　☐ torch　　　☐ regiment
☐ severe　　☐ gunpowder　☐ horror　　☐ fled

TRACK 2-9
p.110~

Part IV: The Rue Plumet IX　プリュメ街 (9)

マリウスはがれきの中に男物の服を着たエポニーヌを発見した。彼女の手には大きな穴が開き胸から血が流れていた。彼女は戦いに彼を巻き込んだのは自分のせいだと言い、コゼットの手紙をマリウスに渡すと息を引き取った。(2分33秒)

キーワード

☐ declare　　☐ crooked　　☐ conflict　　☐ reinforcement
☐ rubble　　☐ pile　　　　　☐ fault　　　☐ deceive

TRACK 2-10
p.113~

Part IV: The Rue Plumet X　ブリュメ街（10）

ジャン・ヴァルジャンへの警告も、コゼットがマリウスへの手紙を託したのもエポニーヌだった。彼女はクールフェラックの家に行き、マリウスを道連れにして死ぬ企みを思いついた。コゼットの手紙を読んでマリウスが書いた手紙はジャン・ヴァルジャンが受け取った。（3分31秒）

キーワード

☐ immediately　　　　☐ heed　　　☐ prowl
☐ suspicion

TRACK 2-11
p.118~

Part V: Jean Valjean I　ジャン・ヴァルジャン（1）

手紙を読んだジャン・ヴァルジャンが銃を買い、バリケードへ向かうと、そこにはスパイ容疑で縛られたジャヴェールがいた。ヴァルジャンは彼の処刑を申し出たが、人目につかないところで彼を解放した。ジャヴェールは後ずさりすると肩を抱え込んで去った。（3分13秒）

キーワード

☐ grim　　　☐ hardened　　　☐ overtake　　　☐ volunteer
☐ entrust　　☐ load　　　　　☐ untie

TRACK 2-12
p.122~

Part V: Jean Valjean II　ジャン・ヴァルジャン（2）

翌日は激しい戦闘になり、マリウスも肩に銃弾を受けたが、ジャン・ヴァルジャンが彼を担いで二人は下水道へ逃れた。出口に着くと門にはカギが掛かっていたが、そこにテナルディエが現れた。彼はヴァルジャンからあるだけの金を奪うと門のカギを開けた。（4分01秒）

キーワード

☐ grate　　☐ slime　　　☐ filth　　　☐ corpse
☐ budge　　☐ anguish　　☐ assassin　☐ slam

TRACK 2-13 p.127~

Part V: Jean Valjean III　ジャン・ヴァルジャン（3）

二人が外にたどり着くと誰かが近づく気配がした。ジャヴェールだった。ジャヴェールは何も言わずにマリウスをジルノルマン家に届け、その後ヴァルジャンの家に向かった。ヴァルジャンが家の踊り場から外を見たとき、ジャヴェールは姿を消していた。（2分45秒）

キーワード

- [ ] willingly
- [ ] hired
- [ ] stir
- [ ] wept
- [ ] roughly
- [ ] landing

TRACK 2-14 p.130~

Part V: Jean Valjean IV　ジャン・ヴァルジャン（4）

ジャヴェールには囚人を解放した自分の行動が我ながら理解できなかった。ジャン・ヴァルジャンの多くの善き行いを振り返ると、罪人ではあるが、畏敬の念を覚えずにいられなかった。彼は頭をセーヌ川に向けると、次の瞬間その人影は暗闇へと飛び込んだ。（2分04秒）

キーワード

- [ ] comprehend
- [ ] condemn
- [ ] repay
- [ ] generosity
- [ ] overwhelm
- [ ] deed
- [ ] crumble
- [ ] railing

TRACK 2-15 p.133~

Part V: Jean Valjean V　ジャン・ヴァルジャン（5）

マリウスの回復は早かった。祖父は、孫が一命をとりとめたことを心から喜び、マリウスの革命思想を許した。ある日、マリウスが父に結婚したいと言うと、祖父は笑いながらそれを許した。二人が誇りを胸に抱きつつわだかまりを捨てた瞬間だった。（1分40秒）

キーワード

- [ ] revolutionism

TRACK 2-16
p.135~

Part V: Jean Valjean VI　ジャン・ヴァルジャン（6）
翌日コゼットとジャン・ヴァルジャン（ムッシュ・フォーシュルヴァン）がマリウスを訪れた。後日彼はコゼットの婚礼資金だと言って大金を持ち込み皆を驚かせた。その後、祖父の書斎はマリウスの弁護士事務所となり、マリウスとコゼットは結婚した。（2分47秒）

キーワード

- [ ] unwrap
- [ ] doubtless
- [ ] withdrawn
- [ ] inherit
- [ ] fortune
- [ ] fade
- [ ] attorney
- [ ] dismay

TRACK 2-17
p.138~

Part V: Jean Valjean VII　ジャン・ヴァルジャン（7）
婚礼の翌日、ジャン・ヴァルジャンはマリウスを訪れ、自分が罪人であることを伝え、コゼットが結婚した今、もう自分の身元を偽ることはできず、家族とかかわることもできないと言った。マリウスは彼が毎晩コゼットに会うことを認めた。（3分27秒）

キーワード

- [ ] radiate
- [ ] celebration
- [ ] conclude
- [ ] sake
- [ ] punishment
- [ ] daytime
- [ ] convince
- [ ] sadden

TRACK 2-18
p.142~

Part V: Jean Valjean VIII　ジャン・ヴァルジャン（8）
マリウスの元に男が訪問して来た。マリウスはすぐにその男がテナルディエだと分かった。彼はジャン・ヴァルジャンは盗人の人殺しだと言って証拠の布切れを見せた。マリウスは自分が探していた命の恩人がヴァルジャンだったことに気づき顔面蒼白となった。（5分55秒）

キーワード

- [ ] murderer
- [ ] portrait
- [ ] fateful
- [ ] sly
- [ ] suicide
- [ ] procure
- [ ] lining
- [ ] stuff

TRACK 2-19
p.148~

Part V: Jean Valjean IX ジャン・ヴァルジャン（9）

ジャン・ヴァルジャンが自分の死期を悟り、最後にコゼットともう一度会いたかったと思ったその時、ドアが開いてコゼットとマリウスが現れた。ヴァルジャンは二人にほほえむと、コゼットに「愛しているよ」と言い、「司祭ならもういるよ」と頭上を指さした。（5分33秒）

キーワード

☐ drag　　☐ repent　　☐ immense　　☐ saint
☐ hush　　☐ stroke　　☐ rightfully　　☐ choke

TRACK 2-20
p.154~

Part V: Jean Valjean X ジャン・ヴァルジャン（10）

パリの貧しい地区にある墓地の人気のない角地の木陰に、人間一人分ぐらいの大きさの石が据えられている。石からは何も読み取ることはできない。（0分38秒）

キーワード

☐ cemetery　　☐ yew　　☐ moss　　☐ entirely
☐ blank

Part I: **Fantine**

I

TRACK 1-1 Just before sunset on an October evening in 1815, a ragged traveler entered a little town. The first place he went was city hall, but he soon came back out to the street. He tried to find lodgings at every inn, but they all turned him away. News and rumors travel fast in a small town. One innkeeper said to the traveler, "We know who you are! You went into city hall, and you showed them an ex-convict's papers! We can't keep a person like you here."

After searching for hours, the tired traveler gave up. Just as he was lying down in the cold street to rest, a kind woman spoke to him. She pointed to a door and told him to try there for something to eat and a place to sleep.

Without much hope, the traveler went to the house and knocked. A kind-looking man opened the door. The traveler did not know that this was the bishop of the town's church. The man welcomed him into his home, but the traveler was tired of pretending. As soon as he stepped inside, his desperation and frustration came out in a hostile outburst.

"Will you really let me stay here?" the traveler demanded. "I am Jean Valjean, an ex-convict who was in jail for nineteen years. I was jailed when I was young because I stole a loaf of bread! We were hungry! My sister had seven little children, and I was trying to feed them! But they arrested me and sentenced me to five years as a galley slave at Toulons. I tried to escape four times and they added years to my sentence. I served a total of nineteen years. Now I'm a free man. Free! But no one will take me!"

Jean Valjean glared at the bishop, who was listening quietly.

"Now that you know who I am and where I come from, will you take me?"

The bishop motioned for the ragged traveler to sit down at his table.

"I will tell the maid to make your bed. Will you join me for supper?"

"What! You won't throw me out?" cried Jean Valjean. "You are a kind man. You're an innkeeper, aren't you?"

"I'm the priest at this church," said the bishop.

"Oh, sir, you are very good!" said Jean Valjean.

The maid brought soup, bread, and wine. Jean Valjean ate this meal as if he had never eaten such delicious food before.

"You have had a long, hard journey," said the bishop when Jean Valjean was done. "You are welcome to rest here for as long as you like."

The bishop showed him to a little guest bedroom. After giving Jean Valjean a candle and some fresh water and towels to wash with, the bishop said good night.

Jean Valjean lay down on the bed. It felt like the most comfortable bed he had ever been in. However, he could not sleep. Jean Valjean was astounded at the kindness of the bishop, but he was troubled by his own future. After this night, he didn't know what he would do. He had to make a life for himself, but how?

Jean Valjean had always been a clever man, but nineteen years in jail made him hard and twisted. Imprisonment and mistreatment had turned his cleverness into cunning. He was only a desperate man when he went into jail, but he had come out a criminal.

Silently, Jean Valjean got out of bed. He had seen a cupboard full of silver plates in the room where he had eaten. He put on his clothes and stepped out of his room. The whole house was quiet. Jean Valjean felt a pang of guilt for what he was about to do.

After all, the bishop had been so kind! He had treated Jean Valjean like a man, and an equal! But Jean Valjean felt he had no choice. He straightened, went to the cupboard, took the silver, and disappeared into the darkness.

The next morning, the bishop heard a knock at his door. There were three policemen there, holding a wretched-looking man. It was the traveler from the night before.

"Sir, we have reason to believe that this thief robbed your house last night!" said one of the policemen. "See here? In his bag he carries silver stamped with the sign of your church!"

"Ah!" cried the bishop. "Jean Valjean, there you are! I'm glad to see you. Look here, you forgot the candlesticks that I gave you! Why did you not take them along with the silver plates? Please, gentlemen, let him go."

Jean Valjean stared at the bishop in shock.

"You mean to say you know this man?" asked a policeman. "And he did not steal from you?"

"Yes, I know him. This silver was a gift. Let him go."

Bewildered, but believing the priest, the police let Jean Valjean go.

With tears welling up in his eyes, Jean Valjean continued to stare at the priest.

"My friend," said the priest, "before you go away, here are the candlesticks. Take them."

Jean Valjean was shaking. He took the candlesticks silently.

"Now, go in peace. And if you should ever come here again, you are always welcome. The door is always open, day and night."

Jean Valjean dropped his head in gratitude and shame.

"Just promise me," said the bishop, "that you will use this silver to become an honest man."

II

TRACK 1-2 A few years later, another traveler—a young woman—came across an inn in Montfermeil, a suburb of Paris. The woman's name was Fantine. She carried her daughter, a beautiful little girl about three years old. There were two children about the same age playing outside the inn. Their mother sat in the doorway, watching.

"What beautiful children," said Fantine to the woman. The two women began to talk.

"Is that your child?" the woman asked.

"Yes, her name is Cosette," said Fantine. "Your inn looks very comfortable."

"Do you want a room?"

"Well, no...But I wonder if you will do me

another service. I am a widow. My husband died recently. I must support my child now, so I am traveling to my hometown of Montreuil-sur-Mer to find work. May I leave my child in your care? I have money to pay you every month, and it would be nice for her to have other children to play with."

The woman narrowed her eyes and thought a moment.

"How much will you pay?"

"I can afford six francs a month."

"Seven," came a voice from inside the inn. A man appeared at the door behind the woman.

"I am Thénardier, and this is my wife. I own this inn. You'll need to pay seven francs a month, plus fifteen more right now for immediate expenses."

"I will pay it," said Fantine.

Fantine never knew what a mistake this was. She was only grateful for the Thénardiers' willingness to help. From that day on, Cosette lived with the Thénardiers, and for four years following, she never had a kind word from anyone. After Fantine left, the Thénardiers treated Cosette like a servant. The money that Fantine sent every month was used on everything but Cosette.

ACK 1-3

In the town of Montreuil-sur-Mer, a man who nobody knew had arrived several years ago and had become a very successful businessman. He went by the name of Monsieur Madeleine. He invented a new clasp that revolutionized the manufacture of a popular type of bracelet. Eventually, he set up his own factory. He was successful, kind, and employed everyone who needed a job. He seemed to always think about others more than himself. He went to church every Sunday. He became very rich but always gave his money away, and he continued to live very simply. The only expensive thing he had in the room where he lived was a pair of silver candlesticks, which were displayed on his mantle.

Monsieur Madeleine was so popular as an employer and a citizen that everyone in the town gradually came to respect and love him, all except one man. His name was Javert, and he was a police inspector. There is in some men the ability to recognize a beast, and he watched Madeleine with suspicious eyes always.

One day, in Montreuil-sur-Mer, a working man was caught under the wheels of his cart. It was old Fauchelevent, the gardener. Monsieur Madeleine was nearby as a crowd gathered. Seeing the old man under the cart, Monsieur Madeleine cried out, "I will give twenty luis to anyone who can lift this cart!"

Nobody stepped forward.

"Come, he is hurt! He may die! Thirty luis, then. Anyone?"

Javert, who was also among the crowd, was watching Madeleine with narrowed eyes.

"I only knew of one man who was strong

enough to lift such a cart," said Javert. "He was a convict at Toulons."

Monsieur Madeleine looked at Javert with startled eyes and seemed to shiver at this statement. But when he looked at the man suffering under the cart, he took off his coat. Madeleine put his broad back under the cart, and, straining with all his might, began to lift it. Others joined to help. They were finally able to get the cart off of Fauchelevent and saved his life. Throughout it all, Javert continued to stare at Madeleine with narrowed eyes.

IV

TRACK 1-4 In 1820, Monsieur Madeleine became the mayor of Montreuil-sur-Mer. Although he refused the request several times, the public wanted him, and he decided to take on the role of a civil servant. This same year, Fantine had left Cosette in Montfermeil with the Thénardiers and had come back to her hometown. She got a job at Mayor Madeleine's factory.

One morning several years later, Mayor Madeleine received a difficult request from Fantine, one of his best employees. She had been ill for about two months, and she was in the hospital. However, just as Mayor Madeleine was sitting down to write his reply to Fantine, Inspector Javert entered the office.

"Sir, I have come here to confess to a crime," said Javert stiffly. He stared straight ahead. "Once I confess, you must dismiss me from my position."

"What do you mean?" asked Madeleine.

"I—I denounced you, sir, to the chief of police in Paris," replied Javert. He faltered for a moment, but he regained his composure and stood very straight.

"What did you say to the chief? Surely, there is no reason for dismissal."

"I must be punished," continued Javert. He looked down now, looking ashamed. "I believed you were a convict. I thought I knew you from the galleys in Toulons, where I worked for many years. I thought you were Jean Valjean, who was released from the galleys in 1815. After his release, he robbed a bishop of a great amount of silver, and the authorities have been trying to catch him ever since."

The mayor turned pale.

"But now I know I was wrong, sir, for the real Jean Valjean has been caught. He faces trial tomorrow."

"Indeed?" replied Madeleine. It was all he could do to remain calm.

"Yes, sir. A man who goes by the name of Champmathieu who was arrested for stealing apples. When he was taken to jail, one of the prisoners recognized him as Jean Valjean, the convict at Toulons. Other prisoners who had been at Toulons recognized him too. Upon hearing this, I went to the jail to see him—and it is true! The man *is* Jean Valjean! He is much older now, but it's him. His trial is tomorrow and I will testify. But first I must apologize for denouncing you, and you must punish me."

Madeleine felt faint. He wanted Javert out of the room.

"Well, I'm very busy at the moment. Go to the trial, Javert, and we shall figure out how to deal with you later. Good day."

Javert left the room. Madeleine sat in silence, utterly shocked, but with a strange calmness coming over him. This man Champmathieu had been caught in a terrible misunderstanding. Jean Valjean could not possibly let another man go to jail for him. No, he would have to confess. There was no other way. This was what God wanted—he could not live this lie anymore.

The next day, to everybody's surprise, Mayor Madeleine came to the trial of Champmathieu. The arrested man did indeed look very much like him, though a bit older. It was easy to see how someone could mistake him for Jean Valjean.

Madeleine had arrived just in time—Javert had already testified and left, and the judge was about to give his ruling. Madeleine interrupted the judge and called out for everyone in the courthouse to look at him.

"You all know me as Mayor Madeleine," he said, "but my real name is Jean Valjean. This man is innocent. Release him. I am the convict at Toulons who stole from the bishop. I belong in jail."

The entire courthouse was so shocked nobody made a sound.

"I will go home to make my preparations. You know where I live. You are welcome to come and arrest me."

With that, Jean Valjean walked out of the courthouse.

V

Jean Valjean knew he had little time to make his preparations before he was arrested. First, he went to the bank and withdrew six-hundred thousand francs, his entire savings. He took this money home. It can be guessed that his intent was to give this money to the poor. Next, he headed to the hospital. One thing that weighed on his mind was the request of Fantine, his employee who was dying. He decided to pay her one last visit.

Jean Valjean arrived at the hospital to find Fantine lying in bed, pale and thin.

"Mayor Madeleine!" she said weakly when she saw him. "Do you have Cosette?"

This was the request Fantine had

made—she had wanted Madeleine to bring back her child from Montfermeil.

Jean Valjean had not been able to go to Montfermeil because of the news Javert had brought him the day before. But he could not bear to disappoint Fantine.

"There now, you must rest," he told Fantine, taking her hand. "Your Cosette is well."

"Oh, you do have her then! When will I see her?"

Seeing the joy in Fantine's eyes, Jean Valjean's heart sank. It was impossible for him to get Cosette before he was arrested. He didn't have enough time. Before he could reply, the door burst open, and Javert strode into Fantine's room.

"Come along!" he yelled at Jean Valjean. His eyes gleamed with triumph, and he grabbed the mayor by the shoulder.

"What is happening, Mayor Madeleine?" asked Fantine, very frightened. "Why are the police here?"

"Inspector Javert," said Jean Valjean as quietly as he could, "you may arrest me, but I ask for just three days. Please, wait three days so I can go to Montfermeil to get this woman's child and place her in good care."

But it wasn't quiet enough—Fantine heard.

"You do not have Cosette?" Fantine's pale face turned absolutely white. All her strength left her, and a single tear rolled down her face.

"I shall not see my child . . ."

She closed her eyes, and with one last breath, Fantine's head fell limply to the side. She was dead.

"Dear God!" cried Jean Valjean. He shook off Javert's hand and went to the dead woman. He said a prayer over her, straightened her body, and crossed her hands over her chest. Then he looked Javert straight in the eyes.

"Take me," he said.

Part II: **Cosette**

I

TRACK
1-6 Jean Valjean became Javert's prisoner, but not for long. After his arrest, he was taken to a local jail to await trial. However, that night, Jean Valjean broke out of prison. He went first to his house but left after several minutes. About an hour later, a man was seen walking from Montreuil-sur-Mer toward Paris, carrying a bundle.

A newspaper dated July 25, 1823, reported that an old, wanted convict by the name of Jean Valjean was arrested but had escaped before trial. The convict had gone under the name of Madeleine and become a rich businessman. Before his arrest, he had apparently taken out a large amount of money from his bank account. He was suspected to have hid the money somewhere, but nobody knew where. The man was currently missing.

However, a few days later in the town of Montfermeil, an innkeeper by the name of Thénardier was paid a visit by a stranger. The stranger was a gentleman about forty years old. He was a large man with broad shoulders, and his hair was turning white. He came with a doll and a new set of black mourning clothes for a little girl. He carried a bag that held two silver candlesticks and another large bundle. He told Thénardier that he was the legal guardian of Cosette, and that her mother had died. He paid the Thénardiers several thousand francs for looking after the girl, and he left with Cosette. She was seven years old.

II

TRACK 1-7 Beyond the old horse market of Paris, down some very dark and lonely streets, there was a building with only one window facing the street. It was here that Jean Valjean brought Cosette to live. Like a bird of prey, he had chosen this lonely place to make his nest.

For some time, Jean Valjean and Cosette were happy. He adored Cosette, and Cosette loved him dearly, for he was kind, and she had never known kindness with the Thénardiers. She loved to go on walks with Jean Valjean and to play with her doll. Jean Valjean mistakenly thought that they were safe.

Jean Valjean was in the habit of going on a walk every evening. He led a very poor, simple life, but he always gave money to others who needed it more. Despite his hidden identity, he strove every day, every hour, to fulfill his promise to the bishop to be a good man.

In Jean Valjean's neighborhood, there was a beggar that sat on the same street every day. Jean Valjean always gave money to this beggar. One day, as Jean Valjean was putting money in his cup as usual, he noticed something strange about the beggar. It was an imposter! Although the man had on the same clothes and sat in the same manner, it was a different man—and he looked like Javert.

That night, Jean Valjean spoke to his landlord and discovered that a new tenant had taken the room next to his. A chill crept up Jean Valjean's spine. He lay awake all night. At one point, he thought he heard someone listening at his door. In that moment, he knew he was no longer safe. He knew that the new tenant must be Javert, who had come to hunt him down.

The next evening, he took Cosette out into the streets on his walk. He tried to hide from her the fact that this was no ordinary walk— they were leaving their home and he was frantically looking for a new place to hide. He knew they had very little time.

Suddenly, Jean Valjean heard the sound of a platoon of soldiers behind them. They quickly turned down an alley, but Valjean caught a glimpse of Javert at the head of the platoon, giving orders to search every door and every corner for Jean Valjean.

There was no time! Jean Valjean's eyes darted here and there, looking for some place— any place—to hide. Far down the street, he saw what looked like a walled garden with no gate—it was in a dark, isolated part of the neighborhood, and he could just make out the tops of trees over the tall wall. He would somehow have to get both Cosette and himself into that quiet place. He grabbed Cosette and looked frantically for a way in. Just then, a rope hanging from a light post caught his eye.

With the sound of the soldiers' footsteps and their shouts coming closer, Jean Valjean quickly cut the rope down and tied it around Cosette. He then tied it around his own waist and scaled the wall.

"Father!" cried Cosette. She was cold, tired, and beginning to realize that something was wrong. She knew they were running from someone.

"Shhh!" replied Jean Valjean when he reached the top of the wall. "Hold on tightly."

He pulled the rope hand over hand, lifting Cosette off the ground and up to the top of the wall. Putting her on his back, he carefully crawled down the wall and dropped into the dark garden. When he landed, a man's voice cried, "Stop! Who are you?"

III

TRACK 1-8 Jean Valjean slowly turned around, holding Cosette. If they weren't allowed to hide in this garden, Javert would certainly catch them. What would happen to Cosette then? He shuddered at the thought.

Desperate, Jean Valjean said, "I'm very sorry, sir, but my daughter and I need to stay here for the night. Please, have pity on us. Please, let us stay."

In the darkness, it was hard to see the man, who was holding up a lantern and studying them.

"My God!" said the man. "Mayor Madeleine! What are you doing here? It's me, don't you remember? Fauchelevent! You saved my life years ago in Montreuil-sur-Mer. You lifted a cart off me!"

A great wave of relief washed over Jean Valjean, and he embraced the man he had once saved.

"Fauchelevent!" he said. "It's good to see you. We have some trouble. I cannot tell you about it, but my daughter is cold and needs a bed. Will you let us stay?"

"You can hide here in the garden for the night, but you can't stay any longer. This is a convent! Only the nuns are allowed to stay here. I'm allowed to stay only because I am their gardener."

Carrying Cosette, Jean Valjean gratefully followed Fauchelevent to a shack where a small bed was set up. After Cosette was asleep, the two men talked.

"We must stay here," said Jean Valjean. "We cannot go back to the city; it is too dangerous for us. I cannot explain why, but remember that I saved your life. You can save ours now by letting us stay."

"I know I owe you my life, and I'd like to help. But it's not up to me. To stay, you have to get permission from the Mother Superior."

"Perhaps you can help me get permission."

Fauchelevent did not get much sleep that night. He was thinking about his old mayor's request. But the next day, with his mind made up, Fauchelevent introduced the former mayor as his brother, Ultimus Fauchelevent, and Cosette as his brother's daughter. After a long conversation, the Mother Superior enrolled Cosette at the convent school and Ultimus Fauchelevent was allowed to stay as an assistant gardener at the convent. They were saved.

Jean Valjean and Cosette found happiness again. Cosette was good at her studies, and she was allowed to visit Jean Valjean every day for an hour. They lived a quiet, content life as the years passed and Cosette grew up.

Part III: **Marius**

I

Marius had lived with his grandfather, Monsieur Gillenormand, and his aunt, Mademoiselle Gillenormand, for as long as he could remember. He had no idea that his father had been a colonel under Napoleon Bonaparte, nor that his father had been given the title of baron for his bravery at war. Indeed, Baron Pontmercy was a war hero whose courage was unrivaled. However, after Napoleon was exiled, the restoration took away his title and pension, and Baron Pontmercy was forced to live as a poor man.

Marius's mother, who was the daughter of Monsieur Gillenormand, died when Marius was still a baby. After her death, Monsieur

Gillenormand decided that he would raise Marius. Monsieur Gillenormand was a wealthy, old bourgeois and royalist. He had plenty of money and important connections to help Marius in life. Monsieur Gillenormand threatened to cut off Marius's significant inheritance if Pontmercy did not give up the boy.

Baron Pontmercy, who loved his son very much, allowed him to be adopted by his grandfather. He knew he could not give Marius the life that Monsieur Gillenormand could. Monsieur Gillenormand, on the other hand, firmly believed that Baron Pontmercy was a traitor and a fool, and more importantly a bad influence on the young boy. He did not ever let Marius see his father.

The first and only time Marius saw his father was when he was eighteen years old. He came home from law school one evening to see his grandfather reading a letter.

"You will travel to Vernon tomorrow," his grandfather said, looking up from the letter.

"Your father is sick."

Marius did as he was told, but when he arrived at his father's house, he realized he was too late. His father lay in his bed, his eyes closed and his hands crossed over his chest. The priest was there, keeping vigil. Baron Pontmercy was dead.

Marius, having never known this dead man, felt very little. The priest handed him a piece of paper, which had a few lines written on it.

"This is for you," said the priest. "Your father talked only of you until the very end."

Marius opened the note. It read, "For my son—The emperor made me a baron upon the battlefield of Waterloo. Since the restoration contests this title which I have bought with my blood, my son will take it and bear it. I need not say that he will be worthy of it."

Marius went back home to Monsieur Gillenormand. He wore some black crepe on his hat for his father. That was all.

II

Marius always went to church on Sunday, and he preferred to go to the church where his aunt had brought him every week as a child. One Sunday a few months after his father's death, Marius went to this church. Being in a rather dreamy mood, he decided to kneel down behind a particular pillar to pray.

Suddenly, a man approached him and said, "My dear sir, you are praying in a special spot."

"What do you mean?" asked Marius.

"Will you allow me to tell you the story? You see, a man who was separated from his son used to come here every Sunday and hide behind this pillar to see his son. He had no other way of seeing him, because the boy had been adopted by his grandfather. The grandfather threatened to disinherit the boy if the father did not give him up, so, the father sacrificed his own happiness so that the boy could have a good life. When he saw his son here every week, he would weep. He loved the boy very much. It was very tragic because the father and son were separated for political reasons—the father had been a colonel for Napoleon, and he had fought bravely at Waterloo. That does not make a man a monster! But the grandfather thought the man was a traitor and would not let him near the boy. The man's name was something like Pontmarie or Montpercy. He had a handsome scar on his face from battle."

"Pontmercy," said Marius, turning pale.

"What? Oh, yes! Pontmercy. Did you know him?"

"He was my father."

The man gave an exclamation of surprise.

Marius offered his arm to the man and walked him home, asking him all about his father.

The next day, Marius said to his grandfather, "I'd like to go on a hunting trip with some friends. May I go away for three days?"

"Four," said his grandfather. "Go. Have fun."

III

Marius was gone for three days, but he wasn't hunting with friends. He went straight to the library of his law school, where he read every newspaper, book, and record he could that mentioned his father or the battle of Waterloo. His father had been a good, noble, brave man. Marius was starting to love the father he never knew. He was also starting to understand his father's politics. All his life, he had taken his grandfather's beliefs as his own opinions. Now he was starting to see things in a different way—to learn a new philosophy.

Marius was gone from home quite often, pursuing this new passion. He also developed a habit of taking flowers to his father's grave.

Back at home, Mademoiselle Gillenormand would wonder out loud to Monsieur Gillenormand, "Where does that boy go all the time?"

Monsieur Gillenormand believed Marius was seeing some girl or another. But Marius was reading, and book by book, Marius shed his old bourgeois skin and his royalism. He gained a passion for the republic, and when he finally became fully revolutionary, he went to a card-maker in town and ordered a hundred name cards that read, "Baron Marius Pontmercy."

Meanwhile, his aunt and grandfather became more and more curious about Marius's mysterious trips.

One day, when Marius returned from one of his trips, his grandfather followed him to his room. Marius took off his coat and the little box he had started to wear around his neck. He laid these on his bed, and he went into the bathroom to take a bath.

His grandfather, stepping into his room, found the box and opened it. There, folded carefully, he found a piece of paper with a few lines written on it. It was Baron Pontmercy's letter to his son, giving him the title of baron. This quite shocked Monsieur Gillenormand, and he continued to search Marius's things. What he found next almost stopped his heart: in Marius's coat pocket, wrapped in blue paper, were one hundred name cards that read "Baron Marius Pontmercy."

When Marius came out of his bath, he found himself facing his grandfather, who was shaking with fury. The two men—one young, one old—fought passionately. Finally, Monsieur Gillenormand said quietly, "A baron like Monsieur and a bourgeois like myself cannot stay under the same roof."

The next day, Marius left his grandfather's house.

IV

Life became stern to Marius. Marius continued to go to school, but without his grandfather's financial support, he was very poor. He lived in a shabby, broken-down apartment and he was hungry most of the time. However, he was very inventive and resourceful. He found ways to make a small loaf of bread last for three meals. Somehow he got through law school, and upon graduation he found work. When Marius discovered that he was able to support himself, he felt a surge of pride. He was still poor, but he was happy that he had taught himself how to survive. He had made his own life for himself.

By the time Marius was twenty years old,

he lived comfortably in a small apartment, and he worked hard to provide for himself. He had two suits: a new one for special occasions, and an old one, which was for every day. He liked to go for a walk in the Luxembourg every afternoon. Marius had become very handsome, and young women turned to look at him when he walked by. But he always assumed they were looking at his old suit and laughing at his frayed collar and sleeves. This made Marius very nervous of women in general. There were only two women in the world that didn't make him nervous. They were his old landlady, and a young girl he barely even noticed.

This young girl walked in the Luxembourg every day with a man whom Marius assumed was her father. The girl wore the shabby, black clothes of a convent school uniform. She seemed about thirteen or fourteen years old, and she was so skinny and pale that she was almost ugly. Her father was a large, powerful-looking man with white hair. Privately, Marius called the girl Mademoiselle Black for her dress and the man Monsieur White for his hair.

At a certain point one year, Marius became very busy with his work and he did not go to the park for many months. Then, finally, he found some free time and was able to stroll along the Luxembourg's avenue of trees again. There he saw Monsieur White walking with a beautiful woman. She wore an elegant black dress and a white hat. She was so striking that Marius got quite confused and nervous. When he stole another look at the young woman, he almost fell over—it was Mademoiselle Black! She was all grown up and so womanly. She must have now been fifteen or so.

"What a difference a summer can make in a young girl's life!" thought Marius. As he stared, almost dumbfounded, at her, the girl looked back at him. She smiled. Marius dropped his eyes and began to sweat. He turned around and quickly walked the other way without quite knowing where he was going.

"She smiled! She smiled!" he thought. Then he looked down at the old suit he was wearing and his heart sank.

"She must be laughing at this shabby suit!" he thought.

The next day, Marius put on his new suit and went to the park. He walked past Mademoiselle Black and Monsieur White. He pretended not to notice them. Then he sat on a bench and pretended to read a newspaper, but really he was staring over the top of it at Mademoiselle Black. In this way, Marius saw the young woman every day, and each day made him fall more in love with her.

V

Meanwhile, Marius was oblivious to the other people in his world, such as the family of four who lived in the room next to his. Their name was Thénardier, and they were very poor—in fact, they were quite miserable.

Several months before, Marius had overheard the landlady saying she was going to evict the family because they had not paid rent in six months. In a moment of compassion, Marius had given her all the money he had to pay their rent. He asked her not to tell the neighbors it was from him, but somehow they found out. In the meantime, busy with his work and the discovery of Mademoiselle Black's transformation, Marius forgot all about them.

One day, Marius heard a knock at his door. It was Eponine, the elder daughter of the Thénardier family. Although she was a pretty girl, she was dirty and thin, and her shirt was ripped.

"Monsieur Marius!" she said with a smile. "I have a letter for you."

And she stepped into his room without an invitation.

Marius opened the letter and read it while Eponine went around his room and looked at his things. The letter was from Eponine's father, Monsieur Thénardier. He thanked Marius for being so generous to his family in the past. Eventually, Marius got to the point of the letter—Thénardier was asking for more money.

Marius gave Eponine five francs. Watching the poor girl made Marius realize that although he was poor, he had never known real misery as this girl had. Eponine went away, and Marius spent the rest of the day thinking about how so many people in the world were as miserable as the Thénardiers. He had heard that the family had once owned an inn in a suburb of Paris, but the inn had failed and the family had no other income.

How cruel life could be, thought Marius.

Pondering these things, Marius noticed a hole in the upper corner of his wall. It looked down into the Thénardiers' room. Unable to control his curiosity, he decided to look into their apartment to see what their lives were like.

VI

As Marius watched, Eponine entered the room. She must have spent some time out in town.

"He is coming! The gentleman is coming!" she cried.

The father stood up.

"How do you know? How did you do it?" he asked.

"I went to church, just like you asked, and I handed him your letter. He read it, then he asked for my address. I told him to follow me, but he said he would go shopping before he came. I came home and waited outside, and I just saw his carriage coming down the street!"

"Good! We must prepare!" said the father.

To Marius's shock, the father threw some water on the fire to put it out, then he kicked the seat off of the only chair in the house. He told his wife to get into bed and act sick. Then he told his younger daughter to break the glass in the window.

"But, father," said the little girl, "I'm afraid."

"Do it, now! Make yourself useful!" yelled the father.

The little girl was more afraid of her father than of broken glass. She put her hand through the glass and cried out. Her hand was bleeding.

"Look what you did!" yelled the mother. "She's hurt herself!"

"Even better!" cried the father. He ripped his shirt to make a bandage for her. An icy wind came through the broken window.

Looking around, the father looked pleased.

"Perfect," he said. "Now we can receive the gentleman."

VII

There was a knock, and Thénardier opened the door. To Marius's great shock, there stood Mademoiselle Black and Monsieur White!

"Thank you so much for coming!" said Thénardier as he welcomed his guests. "You see, we are desperate. We have no fire, and it is cold. Our only chair is broken, my wife is sick in bed, and my youngest hurt her hand at the factory where she works. Now she cannot work, so what will we do? We owe a year's worth of rent…"

Marius knew this was not true because he had already paid six-months' worth for them. But Thénardier went on, listing the family's various miseries.

"I see," said Monsieur White as Mademoiselle Black put a large package on the table. "That package contains some clothes, blankets, and stockings. I hope this will help for now, but I see your situation requires more."

"You are too kind," said Thénardier.

"I only have five francs in my pockets now," said Monsieur White. "Let me take my daughter home. I will come back in the evening at eight o'clock."

Thénardier agreed and the two guests left.

Marius barely knew what to think, but he was overjoyed to see his Mademoiselle Black again. However, he still didn't know her name, or where she lived! Perhaps if he kept watching, he would find something out, he thought.

At eight o'clock, Monsieur White came back with more money as he had promised, and Marius was back at the hole in the wall, watching. But the daughters were not there, the wife was now out of bed, and several strange men entered the room after Monsieur White.

"Do not mind them," Thénardier told Monsieur White. "They are just a few friends of mine."

Suddenly, as Monsieur White placed several hundred francs on the table, Thénardier grabbed his hand.

"Don't you recognize me?" he yelled. "My name is Thénardier! I'm the innkeeper at Montfermeil."

Monsieur White stared at the man and looked all around the room. There were now seven dirty, rough-looking men in the room, yet Monsieur White seemed calm.

"No," he replied.

"You don't know me? Well I knew you as soon as you walked in here! You are the man who came to my inn eight years ago and took Fantine's child! You, dressed like a poor man, you are rich! You are fake, and you took away our help! You child-stealer!"

"I don't know what you mean. I'm not rich; I just try to give what I can. You must have me mistaken for somebody else."

Then, suddenly, Monsieur White shook Thénardier off his arm, jumped to the window, and was almost out of it before the men in the room grabbed him and pulled him back.

"I see now that you are bandits!" said Monsieur White as the men held him. "I gave you money; what else do you want from me?"

"What I need from you is 200,000 francs," said Thénardier. "I know you have it."

He went to the table where a knife lay under a cloth. He grabbed the knife and came close to Monsieur White.

"If you do not give me what I want, I can do bad things to that 'daughter' of yours," he said.

Just then, there was a great crash behind them. Marius shifted his view to see the other side of the room. The door had been broken open, and a tall man was standing there with a crowd of police behind him.

It was Inspector Javert.

"Just as I thought!" cried Javert. "I've been watching this room for bandit activity. You're all under arrest!"

A dozen policemen rushed into the room and arrested the bewildered bandits. But in the commotion, they neglected to arrest one man who slipped out unnoticed through the window. Upon seeing the police, Monsieur White had disappeared.

Part IV:
The Rue Plumet

I

TRACK 2-1 Marius had witnessed the whole thing. He was shocked, but he was quick to take action. The next day, he moved out without leaving a new address. He went to live with his old college friend, Courfeyrac, who shared Marius's revolutionary ideas. Marius still walked in the Luxembourg hoping to see Mademoiselle Black, but he never saw her anymore. He was heartbroken. He had been so close to finding out who she was, but he had lost her, and now he didn't know where to look.

Then, one day in the Luxembourg, he ran into another woman from his past. It was Eponine. She had grown more wretched, but also, strangely more beautiful.

"Oh, Monsieur Marius! I've found you!" she said with joy. "I've looked for you for so long. You left and didn't say where you were going! But now I've found you—it makes me so happy. You look well. Oh, but you have a hole in your shirt! I will mend it for you."

Marius said nothing.

At his cold reception, Eponine darkened.

"You don't seem happy to see me," she said sadly. "I suppose you found out my parents were arrested."

Marius still said nothing.

"But I know something that will make you glad!" Eponine said quickly, almost wildly. "I know where *she* lives. That pretty miss whose father is the philanthropist. They used to walk here, in the Luxembourg. You'd like to know where she lives, wouldn't you? I know you fancy her."

"Yes! Take me there!" said Marius, suddenly coming to life.

Eponine led the way as Marius followed her

to Mademoiselle Black's house.

Along the way, Eponine turned to say, "No, you must not follow so closely. Fall back a few steps. A gentleman like you shouldn't be seen walking with a person like me."

II

After Cosette had finished her education at the convent, Jean Valjean had rented a kind of hidden house that had an entrance on one street, on the Rue Plumet, and another entrance without an address around the corner on the Rue de Babylone. This house and its garden were nestled into the street corner and completely walled off. Whenever they went out, Jean Valjean insisted that they went out the back way, which did not have an address. Ever since the day that he had found Javert posed as a beggar, Jean Valjean had always tried to keep their residence and identity hidden.

Sometime after Jean Valjean and Cosette

moved to the hidden house, Cosette looked in the mirror and realized that she had become pretty. It was a total surprise to her, for it had happened almost overnight. At first it was rather uncomfortable, but she decided to make the best of it. She bought herself some nice clothes and accepted the fact that she was no longer a girl—she was a lady. It was about this time when Marius first saw her again at the Luxembourg.

Jean Valjean had noticed Marius in the Luxembourg. Before, when Cosette was just a schoolgirl, Jean Valjean had not minded this young man. He seemed too stiff and proper, but there was nothing particularly wrong with him. However, one day, he saw Marius look at Cosette in a way that only a man in love would look. And, to Jean Valjean's great surprise, Cosette looked back at the young man in the same way!

Jean Valjean started to despise the young man. It was silly, he knew, but he was jealous.

That was the truth. It upset him that Cosette was always so eager to take their daily walk in the Luxembourg. It was as if she lived for nothing else. Although Jean Valjean knew that he was acting foolish, he stopped walking in the Luxembourg. Cosette did not ask any questions. He was relieved about this. However, he noticed that Cosette was sad. She did not laugh as she used to, and she seemed to become pale and quiet. This broke Jean Valjean's heart. After a few weeks, he asked Cosette if she would like to go to the Luxembourg again. She lit up and said with joy, "Oh, yes!" Jean Valjean felt guilty for having taken away her greatest pleasure.

They went to the Luxembourg that evening, with Cosette chatting all the way there.

However, when they arrived, the young man was not there. Cosette lost some of her cheerfulness, although she continued to chat to be a good companion to Jean Valjean.

The next day, Jean Valjean asked Cosette,

"Would you like to go to the Luxembourg today?"

Cosette, with downcast eyes, said quietly, "No, thank you."

III

One day, as Cosette was walking in the garden at her house, she sat down on a bench close to the iron gate that faced the street. She heard her maid call for her, so she went to the house and returned to the bench in a few minutes. Upon her return, she noticed a large stone that wasn't there before on the bench.

At first, Cosette felt a pang of fear. Who had been here? Was someone in the garden? But she realized it could have been placed by someone outside who stretched his or her arm between the bars of the gate. She picked up the stone and noticed a letter under it. There was no signature or date, but she knew instinctually who it was from and whom it was for. It was from that young man to her! It was a love letter!

Cosette read the letter breathlessly, and when she was done, she kissed the paper. She ran up to her room, locked the door, and spent the night reading and rereading the letter. It made her heart flutter and her face feel hot. The young man expressed how she made him feel, how he had fallen in love with her. She wondered how and when she would hear from this young man again.

It was Jean Valjean's habit to go out for a long walk in the evenings. That evening, when he went out, Cosette arranged her hair in the way that most became her and put on a nice dress. For what? She didn't know what she was doing or what she expected, but she went out to the garden and sat on the bench. After she had been sitting there a while in the moonlight, she felt a presence behind her. She turned to see the young man standing at the gate.

Cosette's heart raced, and she was even a little afraid, but she did not cry out. The young man began to speak.

"Pardon me, I know I shouldn't have come here. I shouldn't disturb you. But my heart will burst if I don't tell you how I feel. Do you recognize me? Do you remember the look you gave me in the Luxembourg one day? I have loved you ever since!"

Cosette felt weak, but also sublimely happy. Not knowing what she was doing, she reached for his hand through the gate and put it over her heart. The young man lit up.

"You love me too, then?"

Cosette let the young man into the garden, and there they talked. When they had finished telling each other everything about themselves, she asked him, "What is your name?"

"My name is Marius. And yours?"

"My name is Cosette."

IV

The lovers were able to meet like this in the garden in the evenings for about six weeks. They were both in heaven. But one day, Cosette changed everything.

"I have to go away," she said. "My father has business and we must go live in England."

Marius felt his whole world shattering.

"No!" he cried. "You cannot!"

Then, feeling quite desperate, he added, "I cannot live without you. I will die if you go away."

"Marius," said Cosette, "come with us! You don't have anything holding you here. You can come to England too!"

"You know I can't do that, for I have no

money!" Then an idea struck Marius and he pulled out his pocket knife. He began to carve something on the garden wall.

"This is my address," he said, "16, Rue de la Verrerie. If anything happens, you should know where I live. I have an idea. I will not come tomorrow as usual, but I will see you the evening after at nine o'clock."

"But what is your idea? Marius, please tell me so I can sleep tonight!"

"You will know later, but I promise you this now: Nothing will separate us."

With that, he left the garden, and Cosette found herself alone, wondering what Marius was thinking.

V

The next day, Jean Valjean was taking a turn at twilight among the trees and shrubs in his garden. He was deeply troubled. Paris was not quiet: political troubles were rocking the city, and people were starting to talk of revolution. Police were starting to inquire into the occupations and identities of suspected revolutionaries throughout the city. It was not a good time to be in hiding. This, coupled with Jean Valjean's discovery of Cosette's love affair, had made him decide to move away from France for good. In less than a week, he hoped to be in England.

When he got close to the bench where Cosette held her secret meetings with Marius, he noticed something written on the wall:

"16, Rue de la Verrerie."

It was a new marking—fresh plaster from the wall dusted the shrubs below. Suddenly, instinctually, Jean Valjean knew exactly what this address was, and what it meant. It could only be *he*, that young man who paraded around and stared at Cosette in the Luxembourg! He had come here, to his home, and Cosette had allowed him in! It was worse than Jean Valjean had suspected: Cosette must truly be in love with that young man.

As Jean Valjean peered through the iron gate, he saw a figure standing on the street just outside. It was a youth, perhaps—too small to be a man, too big to be a boy. The figure flung something over the wall and ran off into the falling darkness. A folded piece of paper landed at Jean Valjean's feet. He picked it up and opened it. There were only three words on it: "Leave this place."

Greatly disturbed, Jean Valjean folded the

paper again and went back to the house. He didn't know who wrote the note or what it meant, but he knew there was no time to waste. He would take action now.

The next evening, Marius came out of Monsieur Gillenormand's house in despair. It was the first time he had seen his grandfather in years. It had taken all the strength he had to enter that house with dignity, but he had done it, and he had spent the evening asking—no, pleading—for his grandfather's permission to marry Cosette. His grandfather had refused on all counts, and Marius was devastated. His great idea had been to get his grandfather's consent and to marry Cosette before her father could take her away to England. But the plan had failed.

For the rest of the night, Marius wandered around Paris feeling numb. Without Cosette, he felt life held nothing for him. With no money or connections with which he could marry Cosette and build a life together, there was nothing he could do—death was the best option for him.

Through his wanderings, he seemed to hear strange sounds in Paris. Coming halfway out of his sad meditations, he wondered now and again, "Are they fighting?"

At nine o'clock, he found himself on the Rue Plumet, in front of Cosette's iron gate. He let himself into the garden, expecting to see Cosette waiting for him on the bench. But she was not there. He looked at the house. All the windows were dark and the shutters closed.

"Cosette?" he called out tentatively.

There was no answer, and he grew bold. He went up to the house and knocked on the door.

"Cosette!" he called. No answer.

In a panic, he cried out again, "Cosette!"

Still no answer. So it was settled. Cosette was gone.

Marius sat down on the steps in front of the door. He smiled sadly, his heart full of tenderness for the time he had shared with this woman who was now gone. He had no regrets, and he had had the happiest six weeks he had ever known. But now, with Cosette gone, there was nothing more for him but to die.

Suddenly he heard a voice at the iron gate.

"Monsieur Marius, is that you?"

Marius rose and saw a figure at the gate.

"Yes," Marius replied. He knew that voice.

"Your friends are expecting you at the barricade, in the Rue de la Chanvrerie."

Yes, that voice sounded rather like Eponine's. Marius rushed through the gate and saw somebody who appeared to be a young man disappear into the twilight.

VI

Meanwhile, at the barricade, the revolutionaries talked in low voices. A dim lamp lit the tables of the wine-shop that served as their headquarters. The lamp threw strange shadows on the great red flag—the sign of the revolutionary—hanging on the wall behind them. The street, and the great barricade they had built to protect it, was dark and silent.

Enjolras, the chief of the revolutionaries, was making his preparations.

"Gavroche," he called to a young boy. "You are small, and nobody will see you. Go out of the barricades and walk by the houses. Look around the streets and tell me what is going on out there."

"Yes, chief!" said Gavroche. "Small people are good for something too!"

VII

As Marius walked toward the Rue de la Chanvrerie, he heard confused sounds—the sound of muskets firing, of distant yelling. But these sounds came rarely. It was a sign that the government was taking its time to gather its forces.

He walked toward the barricade like a man who had accepted his destiny. He had been called, and he must go. Soon, he arrived at the Rue de la Chanvrerie. He saw the great barricade, and the wine-shop where his comrades were. Through the window of the wine-shop, he saw the red flag. Here, Marius stopped, pausing for one moment before he accepted his fate. He thought of Cosette, like a dying man reflecting on the sweetest moments of his life. Suddenly, he heard someone singing an old, traditional folk song in the street.

Enjolras rushed out of the wine-shop.

"It is Gavroche," Enjolras cried to the other men. "He is warning us."

Soon, little Gavroche climbed over the barricade and said, "They are here!"

In a moment, they could hear the sound of rhythmic footsteps in the distance. The revolutionaries all grabbed their arms to prepare for battle. These fifty men would fight against thousands.

There was much less time than they expected—too soon, they heard the footsteps at the barricade. There was a pause. Everyone waited. In the still moment, a soldier called from the other side of the barricade, "Who's there?"

Casting one glance at his men, Enjolras turned to the barricade, lifted his musket, and cried out, "French Revolution!"

"Fire!" came the reply from the other side.

A bright flash washed the whole street in a blue light, and an explosion of bullets blasted the barricade. The street shook, and the red flag in the wine-shop fell.

"Comrades!" cried Enjolras. "Hold strong! Do not waste your gun powder until they enter the barricade!"

In mere moments, the first of the soldiers climbed over the top of the barricade. A brave comrade, Bahorel, fired, killing him, but a second soldier who had just crested the barricade shot Bahorel down. Another soldier sprang down onto Courfeyrac, Marius's college friend.

"Help!" yelled Courfeyrac, while another soldier ran at little Gavroche with his bayonet.

Suddenly, a bullet struck the soldier standing over Courfeyrac in the head, and another bullet sank into the breast of the soldier running at Gavroche. As they died, Courfeyrac and Gavroche turned to see who had saved them. It was Marius.

VIII

TRACK
2-8 Marius had entered the barricade with two pistols. Now that they were both spent, he threw them away and turned toward the wine-shop for more weapons. Just then, a soldier aimed at him, but a hand was laid on the muzzle of the soldier's musket. The soldier fired, and the bullet went through the hand instead of Marius. The wounded person fell, but Marius barely noticed as he rushed into the wine-shop.

Marius saw a keg of powder in a corner, picked it up, grabbed a torch, and climbed in the shadows to one extreme corner of the barricade. He looked down at his comrades who were fighting off the numerous soldiers dropping down from the barricade. On the other side of the barricade, Marius saw a whole regiment of soldiers filling the street. The attack had been faster and more severe than the rebels had expected. Marius knew his friends could not last for long.

Just as the commander was pointing his sword at the barricade to yell "Fire!" again, everyone heard a thundering voice come from above:

"Be gone! Or I will blow up the barricade!"

They all looked up to see Marius standing on top of a wall, holding a torch above his head, his other arm wrapped around a keg of gunpowder.

Everyone looked at him in horror.

"Blow up the barricade, and you will blow yourself up also!" cried a soldier.

"And myself also," answered Marius. He lowered the torch toward the powder. But there was no longer anybody in the street. The soldiers, leaving their dead and wounded, fled and were lost in the night. The barricade was saved.

IX

TRACK 2-9 The rebels celebrated Marius and declared him a chief of the revolution. His friends embraced him and thanked him for joining them. While the rebels cared for the wounded and cleared away the dead, Marius walked through the dark, crooked streets to look at the other, smaller barricades. These had been largely ignored by the government's soldiers, for the main point of conflict had been the great barricade. However, some of the reinforcements had been blown up, and there was rubble here and there. As Marius walked past one pile of broken stones, he heard a weak voice say, "Monsieur Marius!"

He looked down, and there, among the

rubble, was a young man—no, a boy. Marius bent down to the figure and saw it was not a boy but a young woman dressed in men's clothes. It was Eponine!

"What are you doing here?" cried Marius, taking her into his arms.

"I am dying."

Marius was too shocked to reply, but he saw that Eponine's hand had a big black hole in it, and her chest was bleeding as well.

"Oh, God! How were you wounded? Here, I will carry you to the wine-shop. They will dress your wounds."

"Did you see a hand stop the gun that was aimed at you?" asked Eponine weakly.

"Yes…"

"That was mine. The bullet passed through my hand, and it went out through my back. It's too late to dress my wounds. But you can care for me by sitting with me for a while."

"I will stay with you," said Marius, holding her head.

"Monsieur Marius, you thought me ugly, didn't you?"

Marius did not know what to say.

"It's no matter. It's all my fault. I led you here to this battle. But I don't want to deceive you anymore. I have a letter for you in my pocket. Since yesterday. From the pretty miss. She told me to deliver it to you, but I kept it because I didn't want you to have it…Take it."

Trembling, Marius reached into Eponine's pocket and took the letter.

"Now, promise me one thing."

"What, Eponine?"

"Kiss my forehead when I die."

Eponine stared into Marius's eyes, half smiling.

"Do you know? I believe I was a little in love with you."

She smiled again and passed away.

X

Marius kept his promise. He kissed Eponine's forehead, but then his thoughts turned to the letter in his hand. This is the way it is with young lovers. He opened the letter and read: "I'm sorry, my love! My father wants to leave immediately. Tonight we will be in the Rue de l'Homme Armé, No. 7. In a week we will be in England. Cosette."

What had happened was simple: Eponine had done it all. She had dressed in men's clothes. It was she who had given Jean Valjean the message to leave. Jean Valjean had taken heed and told Cosette that evening to pack her things; they would go stay at another house on the Rue de l'Homme Armé, and in a few days they would be in London.

Cosette, devastated by this news, had written to Marius in a hurry. But how would she get the letter to him? She never went out alone, and she could not send her maid. This was when Cosette looked through the gate and saw a youth on the street. It was Eponine, who had been prowling around Cosette's street all evening, hoping that this exact thing would happen. Cosette gave the "youth" five francs and asked him to deliver the letter to 16, Rue de la Verrerie. Eponine put the letter into her pocket.

The next day, Eponine went to Courfeyrac's house not to deliver the letter, but just to see Marius. But Marius was not there, and Courfeyrac told her that all his comrades were going to the barricades that night. She had an idea: she would throw herself into death, and Marius along with her. That evening she went to Cosette's house, where she knew she would find Marius. She knew he would be devastated to find Cosette gone. She told him that his friends were waiting for him at the barricade, and, having nothing left to live for, he had followed her. But, her love for him proved too great to let him die.

Marius now had Cosette's letter, but nothing had changed. He still could not marry her, and she would still go to England. In a hurry, he wrote this letter from a sheet in his notebook:

"My grandfather has refused our marriage, and neither of us have money to start our lives together. I ran to your house, but you were already gone. Now, I go to die, but I will keep my promise to you that nothing will separate us. I will never be far from you. When you read this, my soul will be near you, smiling upon you."

He found Gavroche and told him to take the letter to Mademoiselle Cosette, Rue de l'Homme Armé, No. 7.

Gavroche left right away so that he could

return to the barricade sooner. When he arrived at Rue de l'Homme Armé, he found an older man with white hair sitting outside. It was Jean Valjean, deep in thought.

"Does a Mademoiselle Cosette live here?" asked Gavroche.

"Yes, who wants to know?" replied Jean Valjean with suspicion.

"I have a letter for her from Monsieur Marius, a comrade of the revolution!" said little Gavroche.

Jean Valjean's eyes narrowed.

"I will take the letter to her," said Jean Valjean. But instead, when Gavroche had gone, he opened the letter and read it.

Part V:
Jean Valjean

I

TRACK 2-11 After he had read the letter, Jean Valjean sat still for a long time, thinking. He felt joy—this young man who wanted to take Cosette away was going to die! He would never have to worry about him anymore and Cosette would be safe. But at the same time…He thought about how happy Cosette had been every time they walked in the Luxembourg…

Silently, Jean Valjean put on his coat, went out, bought a gun, and made his way to the barricade.

When Jean Valjean arrived at the rebels' headquarters, he immediately spotted Marius. The young man looked grim, and strong, and hardened. He also saw the little boy who had delivered Cosette's letter. He was pointing to a tall man seated in a dark corner of the wineshop. Jean Valjean recognized that tall man.

"Chief," the boy was saying to one of the rebels, "that man there is a spy."

Enjolras studied the man closely and nodded. Enjolras motioned to three other large men, and they all approached the tall man in the corner.

"Who are you?" Enjolras asked. This direct question may have startled a normal man, but the big man began to smile.

"You are a spy?" continued Enjolras.

"I am an officer of the government," he replied. "My name is Javert."

Enjolras made a motion to the three men, and in a moment they had searched Javert and tied him up.

"Spy," said Enjolras, "you will be shot before the barricade is overtaken."

"If I may," said a voice behind him, "I volunteer to kill the spy."

Everyone turned to see who had spoken. It was a large, older man with white hair. Marius recognized him immediately as Monsieur Fauchelevent, Cosette's father! Javert recognized him too, but as Jean Valjean, the convict.

"Very well," said Enjolras. "I entrust him to you."

Jean Valjean made Javert stand up and led him outside. He found a dark, hidden corner just beyond the barricade. He loaded his pistol as Javert watched him. And then—to Javert's shock—he untied him.

"You are free," said Jean Valjean.

Javert was not a person who was easily surprised. But the shock of this almost made him fall over.

"I don't expect to leave here alive," continued Jean Valjean, "but if I do, I live under the name Ultimus Fauchelevent. I stay at 7, Rue de l'Homme Armé."

Unable to find the words to speak, Javert

slowly backed away, then wrapped his arms around himself and walked off, looking deeply troubled. When Javert had gone, Jean Valjean raised his pistol in the air and shot once. Then, he turned and walked back into the wine-shop.

II

TRACK 2-12 The sun soon came up, and by noon that day, the barricade fell. The heavy fighting left many dead, including Courfeyrac. Marius fought bravely, even with the cuts on his head bleeding into his eyes. As he fought, a bullet struck his shoulder. He fell fainting, but he felt a hand grab him. "I am taken prisoner," was his last thought.

But the hand that had grabbed him was not a soldier's. It was Jean Valjean's. He lifted Marius onto his back and, in the midst of the fighting, carried him from the great barricade down a crooked street. He disappeared around the corner of a house. There, amongst the rubble of a smaller barricade, he saw a hole in the ground with an iron grate over it—a sewer. The damage to the street had left the grate broken, and he could just squeeze himself and Marius down into the hole. This would be their escape. Still carrying the unconscious Marius, Jean Valjean disappeared into the sewer.

It took hours of walking through slime and filth with Marius on his back for Jean Valjean to reach the Grand Sewer. Once there, he could see light at one far end, and he knew there was an exit. He felt a great wave of relief, and he put Marius down to rest for a moment. Marius was still unconscious and losing more blood by the minute, but he was still breathing. Jean Valjean searched Marius's pockets. He found a notebook. Before the battle of the barricade, on the first page of the notebook, Marius had written, "My name is Marius Pontmercy. Carry my corpse to my grandfather's, Monsieur Gillenormand, Rue des Filles du Calvaire, No. 6."

As Jean Valjean rested, he pondered this. Then, with new resolve, he put Marius on his back again and made his way toward the exit. He didn't know someone had been watching him and following him through the sewers.

When he reached the exit, Jean Valjean discovered it was locked. He shook the iron bars of the grate but they wouldn't budge. He had made it this far, but there was no way out! He began to feel that it was all for nothing—that he and this young man would die here in the sewers. And then he thought not of himself, nor of Marius, but of Cosette.

In the middle of his anguish, he heard a voice behind him.

"I have the key."

Jean Valjean turned to see a very thin, very dirty man holding a large key. And he knew the face of the man—it was Thénardier!

However, Thénardier didn't seem to recognize either Jean Valjean or Marius, covered as they were in wounds, blood, and sewer slime.

"I will let you out if you give me half of your earnings," said Thénardier.

"What do you mean?"

"It's clear you're an assassin. No one would carry a dead man through all these sewers unless you want to hide the body. I will let you out so you can hide the body, and I won't say anything about this to anyone. Just give me half of what you earned to kill this man."

Silently, Jean Valjean searched through his pockets for money. Meanwhile, Thénardier bent down and ripped a strip of cloth out of Marius's coat to report a murder—for a reward, of course—and to have something to show as evidence. Jean Valjean did not notice him doing this.

After much searching, Jean Valjean came up with only thirty-two francs.

"You didn't kill him for very much, did you?" said Thénardier, and he took all the money instead of half.

Thénardier opened the gate as Jean Valjean

picked up Marius again. As soon as they were out, Thénardier slammed the gate shut, locked it, and disappeared back into the sewers.

III

They were outside! At Jean Valjean's feet was a little river, the water of which fed into the sewer. Jean Valjean stooped before the river, let Marius down, and poured a handful of water onto Marius's face. As he was involved in this task, he felt a presence approach him. He looked up. It was Javert!

"Jean Valjean," said Javert grimly as he grabbed the ex-convict by the shoulders.

"Inspector Javert," he said, "I am your prisoner. I gave you my address last night so that you could find me if I lived. I'll go with you willingly, but please help me do one thing. Help me take this young man, who is dying, to his grandfather's house."

Javert seemed to be listening. He looked at Marius and said to himself, "This man was in the barricade…This is the one they called Marius."

Javert looked at Jean Valjean.

"He is wounded," Javert said. "You brought him here from the barricade?"

"He must go to his grandfather's," said Jean Valjean, and showed him the message in Marius's notebook.

Javert was silent. But a minute later, he was traveling in a hired carriage with the two men to the Rue des Filles du Calvaire.

When they arrived at the grandfather's house, Javert knocked and said in his most official tone, "I must speak to Monsieur Gillenormand. His son has been brought home. He is dead."

These words caused a great stir in the great house. Marius was taken immediately to a bed, a doctor was called, and the grandfather came rushing into the room where Marius lay.

Seeing his grandson, Monsieur Gillenormand fell to his knees and wept.

Javert left unnoticed from this scene and returned to his prisoner, Jean Valjean, who was waiting for him in the carriage.

"Inspector Javert," said Jean Valjean, "please allow me to go home to say good bye. Then do with me what you will."

Javert was silent for a moment. Then he nodded and told the driver, "Go to 7, Rue de l'Homme Armé!"

When they reached Jean Valjean's house, they both exited the carriage.

"Very well," said Javert roughly. "Go up. I will wait here."

Jean Valjean turned and entered his house. He went up the stairs. When he reached the landing, he looked out the window, and his eyes grew wide at what he saw—or rather, what he didn't see.

Javert was gone.

IV

TRACK 2-14 Slowly, without quite knowing what he was doing, Javert had turned and walked away from the Rue de l'Homme Armé. He walked with his head down, deep in thought. Whether he knew it or not, he was heading toward the Seine River.

Javert had just done something he couldn't comprehend. He had let a prisoner go. But at the same time something in him had not let him condemn a man who had saved his life. He felt that Jean Valjean had done him a favor, and according to his principles, he had to repay that favor. But this, he thought, shuddering, put him on the same level as a convict—he owed his life to a convict and he had repaid it by letting the convict go. How could this be? Who was Javert? He searched hard but couldn't find himself anymore.

Jean Valjean greatly confused him. The convict's generosity overwhelmed him. He thought of him as Mayor Madeleine and all the good deeds he had done. He was a criminal, and yet Javert found himself respecting him. This was horrible; this he could not live with. He felt all the principles that had shaped and guided his life crumble away—they did not mean anything anymore!

By this time Javert had reached the Seine. He stood on a bridge, looking down into the shadows of the water. There were only two ways out of this philosophical problem: Go back to Jean Valjean and return the criminal to prison. Or…

Suddenly, Javert took off his hat and laid it on the railing of the bridge. A moment later, a tall, dark figure could be seen standing on the edge of the bridge, bent toward the Seine. A moment more, and the figure sprang into the darkness. There was a splash, and then there was nothing.

V

-15 Marius recovered quickly. He was young, he had a good doctor, and luckily, no bullets remained inside him. However, he was still a rebel, and his grandfather was still a royalist. Marius felt that his grandfather was waiting for the right moment to denounce his actions. As he recovered, he prepared for the fight he thought he would have with Monsieur Gillenormand.

What Marius did not realize was that his grandfather loved him more than he loved his politics. Monsieur Gillenormand was so overjoyed to have his grandson alive, safe, and recovering that he had quite forgiven Marius of his revolutionism. All he wanted was for

Marius to be healthy again.

With this in mind, one day Monsieur Gillenormand said to Marius, "My dear boy, perhaps it is time for you to eat meat instead of fish. Fried fish is perfect for a man early in his recovery, but meat will put you back on your feet."

Marius glared at his grandfather and said, "That leads me to say something to you."

"What is it?"

"I wish to marry."

"Of course!" said his grandfather, laughing. "And you shall!"

Shocked, Marius cried out, "Really, grandfather?"

"Yes, you shall see her tomorrow if you wish!"

Marius saw the love in his grandfather's eyes and realized he had been wrong. The two men embraced. It was a moment that neither man, despite their pride, ever forgot.

VI

The next day Cosette and Jean Valjean visited Marius. The two lovers were overwhelmed with happiness to see each other again. As the old people looked on, Cosette wept with joy while Marius told her of his plans for their future lives together.

From that day on, Cosette and Monsieur Fauchelevent came to visit Marius everyday. On one of these days, Monsieur Fauchelevent revealed a secret that astounded everyone.

He brought with him a large bundle under his arm.

"This is Cosette's," he said, as he unwrapped the bundle. Inside were hundreds of hundred-franc notes. "There are six-hundred thousand francs here, and it has been left to Cosette to claim on her wedding day."

The reader will doubtless remember that many years ago, on the night of his arrest, Jean Valjean had visited his bank and withdrawn all the money in his account. After his escape from the local jail, Jean Valjean had buried that money somewhere along the way to get Cosette in Montfermeil. This was the money he showed now. To protect Cosette's identity and to keep his own identity a secret, he explained that Cosette was not his daughter but the daughter of another Fauchelevent. Her family was now all dead, and only Cosette remained. She would inherit the Fauchelevent family fortune when she was married. Having been a mayor, Jean Valjean was familiar with all the paperwork this required, and the whole thing was very easy.

Cosette was very sad to discover that Jean Valjean, known to her and to all as Ultimus Fauchelevent, was not her father. At any other time of her life, this would have broken her heart, but at the moment she was filled with joy. She had Marius. The young man came, and the old man faded away. Such is life. She continued, however, to call Monsieur Fauchelevent father.

It was arranged for the couple to live with Monsieur Gillenormand. He insisted on giving them his own room—the finest in the house. He was absolutely taken with Cosette, and he happily busied himself filling the room with nice furniture. The grandfather's library was given to Marius as an attorney's office.

Marius and Cosette were married on February 16, 1833. It was a white, snowy night, and the wedding, blessed as it was by true happiness, was perfect.

The next day, however, filled Marius with shock and dismay.

VII

TRACK 2-17 Jean Valjean woke in his bed on the Rue de l'Homme Armé the day after the wedding knowing what he had to do. He dressed himself slowly, preparing himself for what he would say. He walked to Monsieur Gillenormand's house and asked to see Marius alone.

"Father!" cried Marius when he saw Jean Valjean. He seemed to radiate joy. "What a perfect day we had yesterday! I am glad to see you, but why so early? Surely you wanted some more time in bed after our celebrations last night?"

"I must tell you something," said Jean Valjean, "because you are Cosette's husband

and I must not keep the truth from you. My name is Jean Valjean, and I am a criminal."

Jean Valjean explained to Marius that he had been a convict at the galleys in Toulons, and that he had been put there for stealing. Marius listened to it all without moving or making a sound. He stood in complete shock.

"And so," concluded Jean Valjean, "I do not want to dirty your house, nor do I want to lie to your family. I lied about who I was when I was Cosette's guardian, because it was for Cosette's sake. But now Cosette is married and she is taken care of. Now I cannot lie about who I am, and it is not good for you that I am associated with your family."

He paused.

"But please promise not to tell Cosette. I—I can handle any punishment but that."

Marius promised.

"Now that you know what I am, tell me, do you think Cosette should still see me?"

As a husband, Marius felt a duty to protect

his wife. This was his strongest feeling, and he replied, "No, I don't think it would be good for her to have you near."

Jean Valjean dropped his head.

Feeling some pity, Marius added, "But perhaps you can come see her here every evening."

"Yes, thank you," said Jean Valjean with tears of happiness. "I shall come tomorrow."

And so began the daily visits of Jean Valjean. Cosette did not understand why her father would not come to live with her and Marius, and why he did not come visit in the daytime, only in the evenings. She tried to convince him to change his ways, but he always refused, and in the end, Cosette decided to let her father have his way. She did not complain.

For a while, Jean Valjean came every evening. However, gradually, the visits became less frequent, and one day Jean Valjean stopped coming at all. Cosette, though saddened by this, was busy with the engagements of her new life. She thought her father must have his own reasons for not coming, and she did not ask questions.

Jean Valjean had decided not to disturb the happy couple with his presence anymore. Being away from Cosette made him miserable, but he accepted this. It was best for Cosette if hc stayed away. So he sat in his room. He soon found he was becoming very weak. If a doctor had seen Jean Valjean, he would have said that he was dying of a broken heart.

VIII

Meanwhile, although the young people were happy together, Cosette was sad that she didn't see her father, and Marius was troubled by what he knew about Jean Valjean. He tried researching Jean Valjean's past, but all he could find out was that more than ten years ago, he took out six-hundred thousand francs from the account of a Monsieur Madeleine, a popular mayor of Montreuil-sur-Mer. He also remembered the night of the battle of the barricade, when he saw Jean Valjean take the policeman, Javert, outside. He had heard the gun go off. This made him a murderer in addition to a robber, and Marius shuddered at the thought of such a man being near his dear Cosette.

However, all things come to an end, and this portrait of Jean Valjean changed one fateful day.

Marius was in his office when his servant entered to tell him a man had come to see him. It was a man by the name of Thénard. Marius put down his pen.

"Tell him to enter."

In came Thénardier. Marius recognized him immediately, but he only said, "How can I help you?"

"Sir, I'm sorry to disturb you. My name is Thénard, and I have some very important information to tell you," he said with a sly look. "It is information that could harm your family. It pertains to your wife's father. Of course, I want to tell you from the goodness of my heart, but you see, I'm a poor man and all I ask is twenty thousand francs in repayment for my information."

Marius stood up.

"I know you," he said. "Your name is really

Thénardier. I also know the information you want to tell me. I have no need for you. Please go."

"You don't know this information! The father of your wife is a criminal—a robber and an assassin! I will tell you more if you pay me."

"Enough! He told me that himself! His name is Jean Valjean, and he escaped from prison. I know he is a robber because he took six hundred thousand francs from a man named Madeleine. He gave it to my wife, but neither she nor I have touched it. It is dirty money. I know he is an assassin because he killed the police officer, Javert."

At this, Thénardier began to smile. He had the look of someone who had just won a game.

"You are wrong, sir," said Thénardier. "Jean Valjean never robbed Monsieur Madeleine because he *was* Monsieur Madeleine. He never killed Javert, because Javert killed himself. I have proof."

Thénardier showed him two old, yellowed newspaper clippings. The first established the identity of Jean Valjean as Monsieur Madeleine. The second was a report on the suicide of police inspector Javert.

"Goodness! Oh!" cried Marius. "Then this man is not a robber but a hero!"

"You are wrong again, sir," said Thénardier. "I have proof of this as well."

With this, he pulled out a strip of cloth from his pocket. Showing it to Marius, Thénardier said, "Because I fell on hard times, I procured the key to a sewer and lived there for several months. It was my only shelter. On June 6, 1832, the day of the battle of the barricade, I saw a man—Jean Valjean—carry through the sewers a young, rich man. The young man was dead! Now, nobody would carry a corpse through the filthy and dangerous sewers unless they meant to hide the body! And nobody would hide a body unless they were responsible for the death! I know, sir, that Jean Valjean must have killed that young man to steal his money! He is a robber and a murderer! Here, I have proof: this strip of cloth came from the young man's coat!"

While Thénardier was talking, Marius was turning white. Ever since his recovery, he had been trying to find the man who had saved him. He remembered being shot by the barricade and a hand grabbing him as he fell. But he remembered nothing else until he awoke in his grandfather's house. The servants could only say that a police officer had delivered him to his grandfather's house, and that there appeared to be another man in the carriage, but nobody had looked closely.

If Thénardier's story was true, it was Jean Valjean who had saved his life! He had been there, at the barricade, fighting alongside him! He had carried him through the sewer—certainly not for himself, for what did he care if Marius lived or died? No, he had carried him through the sewer and saved his life for Cosette!

Marius rushed to a closet, where he pulled out a dirty coat.

"Thénardier," he said, "look."

Marius exposed the inside of the coat, where a strip of the interior lining was missing. He took the strip from Thénardier and fitted it to the lining: it was a perfect fit.

"I was the young man you saw Jean Valjean carry through the sewer! He did not rob me; he saved my life! Here!"

He stuffed several thousand francs in Thénardier's hand.

"Take this and go! Leave us alone, and let us never see you again!"

Thénardier, who was now the shocked one, took the money and left forever.

"Oh, god!" cried Marius. "Cosette! Cosette! We must see your father now! Hurry!"

IX

TRACK 2-19 That morning, Jean Valjean had found that he could not get out of bed. His legs would not move. With great effort, he dragged himself out, and he fell on the floor.

"So," he thought, "my time has come. I will die today."

The room was cold, and Jean Valjean did not have the strength to light a fire. It was all he could do to get off the floor and sink into a chair. The thought of dying alone, in this cold room, without seeing Cosette one last time brought tears to his eyes. He had done all he could to repent for his past deeds. He thought of the bishop who had saved him long ago, and he reflected on all the sacrifices he had made to try to be a good man. And for all his sacrifices, he could not have the one thing that mattered to him: to see Cosette again.

"Oh!" he thought. "If I could just see Cosette again, I could die happily...But I fear it is too late..."

Just then there was a knock on the door.

"Come in," he said weakly.

The door opened. Cosette and Marius appeared.

Cosette rushed into the room.

"Cosette!" cried Jean Valjean, and he rose from his chair in a burst of strength, his arms stretched out and trembling.

Cosette threw herself into his arms.

"Father!" she cried. They sat. There was immense joy in Jean Valjean's eyes.

"Cosette! Is it really you, Cosette? Oh, my God!"

Jean Valjean looked at Marius and said, "And you too, forgive me?"

Then, he added, "Thank you."

"Oh, do not thank me!" cried Marius. "You are the one who should be thanked! You, who saved my life for Cosette's sake, who carried me through battle and through the sewers! You who were a generous and fair mayor! You who saved Javert's life! You who protected Cosette! Oh, Cosette, I owe this man everything, and he is the one who thanks me? He is a saint!"

"Hush, hush," said Jean Valjean, "why tell all that?"

"But you!" exclaimed Marius, "why did you not tell it? You save people's lives and you hide it from them! You do harm by hiding your good deeds from the world!"

"No, I told the truth."

"Not the whole truth!" replied Marius. "I owed my life to you, why did you not say so?"

"Because I felt that you were right," said Jean Valjean. "It was necessary that I go away. I did not want to bring shame or danger to Cosette, or to you and your family."

"You are her father and mine," said Marius, holding the old man's hand. "You will come and live with us for the rest of your days!"

Jean Valjean smiled.

"That is good, thank you. But soon, I shall not be here," he said, stroking Cosette's hair.

"Oh! His hands are so cold!" said Cosette. "Father, are you sick? Are you suffering?"

"No, no," said Jean Valjean. "I am very happy. Only—"

"What?"

"I shall die in a few minutes. But I have something important to tell you. It makes me sad that you have not used your money, Cosette. It is rightfully yours. I earned that money by inventing a cheaper and better way to make bracelets. I will tell you the details to put your minds at rest."

He explained his invention to the couple, and they realized that he had earned every franc.

"Please," said Jean Valjean, "believe me,

that money is not stolen; it is yours."

He smiled at them both.

"I love you," he told Cosette, and he kissed her hand. He looked at Marius and said, "I love you too. I believe you make Cosette happy. Please take good care of her."

"Oh, father!" cried Cosette. "You grow so cold! Do you need a priest?"

"I have one," said Jean Valjean.

And, with his finger, he pointed above his head, where he seemed to see someone. Perhaps the good bishop was watching over Jean Valjean after all.

"Come closer, my children," said Jean Valjean in a whisper. "Cosette, I want you to have my two silver candlesticks. I hope the person who gave them to me is satisfied with me. My children, remember that I am a poor man. I want to be buried with just a stone to mark the spot. Put no name on the stone. That is my wish. And Cosette, you should know your mother's name. It was Fantine. She suffered much and loved you very much. I am going away now, children. Love each other dearly, for that is all that matters in life: to love. I die happy."

Cosette and Marius fell to their knees, choked with tears. They each took one of the old man's hands and held it tightly. Jean Valjean looked up to heaven, and his old hands moved no more.

X

In the cemetery of Père Lachaise, near one of the poor neighborhoods of Paris, there is a great yew tree in a lonely corner. Among the grass and the moss, in the shade of the tree, there is a stone. It is not protected from the elements. The air turns it black, the moss turns it green, and the birds stop there to rest. The stone is long enough and narrow enough to cover a man, but it is entirely blank. No name can be read there.

Word List

- 語形が規則変化する語の見出しは原形で示しています。不規則変化語は本文中で使われている形になっています。

- 一般的な意味を紹介していますので、一部の語で本文で実際に使われている品詞や意味と合っていないことがあります。

- 品詞は以下のように示しています。

名名詞	代代名詞	形形容詞	副副詞	動動詞	助助動詞
前前置詞	接接続詞	間間投詞	冠冠詞	略略語	俗俗語
熟熟語	頭接頭語	尾接尾語	記記号	関関係代名詞

A

- **ability** 名できること, (~する) 能力

- **about to** 《be –》まさに~しようとしている, ~するところだ

- **absolutely** 副完全に, 確実に

- **accept** 動①受け入れる ②同意する, 認める

- **according to** ~によれば [よると]

- **account** 名勘定, 預金口座

- **across** 熟 come across ~をふと見つける

- **act** 動①行動する ②演じる

- **activity** 名活動, 活気

- **add** 動①加える, 足す ②足し算をする ③言い添える

- **addition** 名①付加, 追加, 添加 ②足し算 in addition 加えて, さらに

- **address** 名住所, アドレス

- **adopt** 動~を養子 [養女] にする

- **adore** 動熱愛する, 崇拝する

- **affair** 名事柄, 事件 love affair 恋愛

- **afford** 動《can –》~することができる, ~する (経済的・時間的な) 余裕がある

- **after all** やはり, 結局

- **ah** 間《驚き・悲しみ・賞賛などを表して》ああ, やっぱり

- **aim** 動①(武器・カメラなどを) 向ける ②ねらう, 目指す

- **all** 熟 after all やはり, 結局 all for nothing むだに all one's life ずっと, 生まれてから at all まったく~ない for all ~ ~にもかかわらず on all counts あらゆる面 [点] で

- **alley** 名路地, 裏通り, 小道

- **allow** 動①許す, 《 – … to ~》…が~するのを可能にする, …に~させておく ②与える

- **alone** 熟 leave ~ alone ~をそっとしておく

- **along the way** 途中で, これまでに

□ **along with** ～と一緒に

□ **alongside** 前 ～のそばに，～と並んで

□ **although** 接 ～だけれども，～にもかかわらず，たとえ～でも

□ **amongst** 前 の間に［を・で］

□ **amount** 名 量，額

□ **anguish** 名 苦悩，苦悶

□ **anybody** 代 ①《疑問文・条件節で》誰か ②《否定文で》誰も（～ない）③《肯定文で》誰でも

□ **anymore** 副 《通例否定文，疑問文で》今はもう，これ以上，これから

□ **anyone** 代 ①《疑問文・条件節で》誰か ②《否定文で》誰も（～ない）③《肯定文で》誰でも

□ **apartment** 名 アパート

□ **apologize** 動 謝る，わびる

□ **apparently** 副 見たところ～らしい，明らかに

□ **appear** 動 ①現れる，見えてくる ②（～のように）見える，～らしい appear to ～するように見える

□ **approach** 動 接近する

□ **arrange** 動 ①並べる，整える ②取り決める ③準備する，手はずを整える

□ **arrest** 動 逮捕する 名 逮捕 under arrest 逮捕されて

□ **as** 熟 as ～ as one can できる限り～ as if あたかも～のように，まるで～みたいに as long as ～する以上は，～である限りは as soon as ～するとすぐ，～するや否や as usual いつものように，相変わらず as well なお，その上，同様に just as（ちょうど）であろうとおり such as たとえば～，～のような the same ～ as … …と同じ（ような）～

□ **ashamed** 形 恥じた，気が引けた，《be – of ～》～が恥ずかしい，～を恥じている

□ **ask ~ if** ～かどうか尋ねる

□ **asleep** 形 眠って（いる状態の）

□ **assassin** 名 暗殺者

□ **assistant** 名 助手，補佐

□ **associate** 動 ①連合［共同］する，提携する ②～を連想する ③交際する

□ **assume** 動 ①仮定する，当然のことと思う ②引き受ける

□ **astound** 動 仰天させる，驚かせる

□ **at first** 最初は，初めのうちは

□ **attack** 名 攻撃

□ **attorney** 名 弁護士，法定弁護人

□ **authority** 名 ①権威，権力，権限 ②《the -ties》（関係）当局

□ **avenue** 名 並木道

□ **await** 動 待つ，待ち受ける

□ **awake** 形 目が覚めて

□ **away** 熟 pass away 死ぬ right away すぐに

□ **awoke** 動 awake（目覚めさせる）の過去

B

□ **back** 名 背中 副 戻って，後方へ，後ろに 動 後退する back away 後ずさる，腰が引ける

□ **Bahorel** 名 バオレル《人名》

□ **bandage** 名 包帯

□ **bandit** 名 強盗，詐欺師

□ **bar** 名 棒，かんぬき

□ **barely** 副 ①かろうじて，やっと ②ほぼ，もう少しで

☐ **baron** 名男爵

☐ **barricade** 名バリケード, 障害物

☐ **bath** 熟 take a bath 風呂に入る

☐ **bathroom** 名①浴室 ②手洗い, トイレ

☐ **battle** 名戦闘, 戦い

☐ **battlefield** 名戦場

☐ **bayonet** 名銃剣

☐ **bear** 動耐える

☐ **beast** 名けだもの(のような人物)

☐ **because of** ～のために, ～の理由で

☐ **bed** 熟 be sick in bed 病気で寝ている get into bed ベッドに入る get out of bed 起きる, 寝床を離れる

☐ **bedroom** 名寝室

☐ **before** 熟 the night before 前の晩

☐ **beggar** 名乞食, 物貰い

☐ **behind** 前①～の後ろに, ～の背後に ②～に遅れて, ～に劣って

☐ **belief** 名信じること, 信念, 信用

☐ **belong** 動《 – to ～》～に属する, ～のものである

☐ **below** 副下に[へ]

☐ **bench** 名ベンチ, 長いす

☐ **bend** 動曲がる, 曲げる bend down かがむ, 腰を曲げる

☐ **bent** 動 bend (曲がる)の過去, 過去分詞

☐ **better** 熟 even better さらに素晴らしいことに

☐ **bewilder** 動当惑させる, まごつかせる

☐ **beyond** 前～を越えて, ～の向こうに

☐ **bird of prey** 猛禽類

☐ **bishop** 名司教, 主教

☐ **bit** 名①小片, 少量 ②《 a – 》少し, ちょっと

☐ **blank** 形何も書いていない, 無記名の

☐ **blanket** 名毛布

☐ **blast** 動爆破する

☐ **bleed** 動出血する, 血を流す[流させる]

☐ **blessed** 形祝福された, 恵まれた

☐ **blood** 名血, 血液

☐ **blow** 動①(風が)吹く, (風が) ～を吹き飛ばす ②破裂する blow up 爆破する[させる]

☐ **blown** 動 blow (吹く)の過去分詞

☐ **bold** 形勇敢な, 大胆な, 奔放な

☐ **bourgeois** 名ブルジョア, 中産階級の人

☐ **bracelet** 名ブレスレット

☐ **brave** 形勇敢な

☐ **bravely** 副勇敢に(も)

☐ **bravery** 名勇敢さ, 勇気ある行動

☐ **break open** (金庫などを)こじ開ける

☐ **break out of** ～から脱出する, 脱走する

☐ **breast** 名胸, 乳房

☐ **breath** 名息, 呼吸

☐ **breathe** 動呼吸する

☐ **breathlessly** 副ハラハラしながら, 息せき切って

☐ **bring back** 戻す, 呼び戻す

☐ **bring home** 家に持ってくる

☐ **broad** 形幅の広い

☐ **broken-down** 形ぼろぼろの, 壊れている

☐ **budge** 動少し動く[動かす], 微動す

る

□ **building** 名建物, 建造物, ビルディ
ング

□ **bullet** 名銃弾

□ **bundle** 名束, 包み

□ **burst** 動①爆発する[させる] ②破
裂する[させる] 名破裂, 爆発

□ **bury** 動埋葬する, 埋める

□ **businessman** 名ビジネスマン, 実
業家

□ **busy with** 《a – 》～で忙しい

□ **but** 熟not ～ but … ～ではなくて
…

□ **by this time** この時までに, もうす
でに

C

□ **call for** ～を呼び求める, 呼び出す

□ **call out** 叫ぶ, 呼び出す, 声を掛ける

□ **call to** ～に声をかける

□ **calm** 形穏やかな, 落ち着いた

□ **calmness** 名静けさ

□ **can** 熟as ～ as one can できる限
り～

□ **candle** 名ろうそく

□ **candlestick** 名ろうそく立て

□ **card-maker** 名名刺屋

□ **care** 熟care for ～の世話をする, ～
を扱う take care of ～の世話をする,
～の面倒を見る, ～を管理する take
good care of ～を大事に扱う, 大切
にする

□ **carriage** 名馬車

□ **cart** 名荷馬車, 荷車

□ **carve** 動彫る, 彫刻する

□ **cast** 動投げる

□ **catch a glimpse of** ～をちらっと
見る, 垣間見る

□ **celebrate** 動祝う, 祝福する

□ **celebration** 名①祝賀 ②祝典,
儀式

□ **cemetery** 名共同墓地

□ **certain** 形ある

□ **certainly** 副確かに, 必ず

□ **Champmathieu** 名シャンマティ
ュー《人名》

□ **chat** 動おしゃべりをする, 談笑する

□ **cheerfulness** 名明るさ, 快活さ

□ **chest** 名胸

□ **chief** 名頭, 長, 親分

□ **child-stealer** 名子供泥棒, 人さら
い

□ **chill** 名冷え, 身にしみる寒さ

□ **choice** 名選択(の範囲・自由)

□ **choke** 動①息が詰まる, 窒息する
②つかえる

□ **citizen** 名市民, 住民

□ **civil** 形①一般人の, 民間(人)の
②国内の, 国家の civil servant 公務
員

□ **claim** 動①主張する ②要求する,
請求する

□ **clasp** 名留め金

□ **clear** 形はっきりした, 明白な clear
away ～を片付ける

□ **clever** 形頭のよい, 利口な

□ **cleverness** 名賢さ

□ **climb over** ～を乗り越える

□ **clipping** 名切り抜き, クリッピング

□ **close** 熟be close to ～に近い get
close to ～に近づく, 接近する

A B C D E F G H I J K L M N O P Q R S T U V W X Y Z

A
B
C
D
E
F
G
H
I
J
K
L
M
N
O
P
Q
R
S
T
U
V
W
X
Y
Z

☐ **closely** 副 ①密接に ②念入りに, 詳しく ③ぴったりと

☐ **closet** 名 戸棚, 物置, 押し入れ

☐ **collar** 名 えり

☐ **colonel** 名 大佐

☐ **come** 熟 come across 〜をふと見つける come along 一緒に来る, ついて来る come back 戻る come back to 〜へ帰ってくる, 〜に戻る come down 下りて来る come in 中にはいる, やってくる, 出回る come out 出てくる, 出掛ける, 姿を現す come out of 〜から出てくる, 〜をうまく乗り越える come over やって来る, 〜の身にふりかかる come through 通り抜ける come to life 目覚める, 復活する come up 浮上する come up with 見つけ出す

☐ **comfortable** 形 快適な, 心地いい

☐ **comfortably** 副 心地よく, くつろいで

☐ **commander** 名 司令官, 指揮官

☐ **commotion** 名 ①激動 ②騒動, 騒ぎ

☐ **companion** 名 友, 仲間, 連れ

☐ **compassion** 名 思いやり, 深い同情

☐ **complain** 動 ①不平 [苦情] を言う, ぶつぶつ言う ②(病状などを) 訴える

☐ **complete** 形 完全な, まったくの

☐ **completely** 副 完全に, すっかり

☐ **composure** 名 平静, 落ち着き

☐ **comprehend** 動 ①よく理解する ②包含する

☐ **comrade** 名 (通例男性の) 仲間, 同僚, 同志

☐ **conclude** 動 ①終える, 完結する ②結論を下す

☐ **condemn** 動 ①責める ②有罪と判決する

☐ **confess** 動 (隠し事などを) 告白する, 打ち明ける, 白状する

☐ **conflict** 名 ①不一致, 衝突 ②争い, 対立 ③論争

☐ **confuse** 動 困惑させる, 混乱させる

☐ **confused** 形 困惑した, 混乱した

☐ **connection** 名 つながり, 関係故

☐ **consent** 名 同意, 承諾, 許可

☐ **contain** 動 含む, 入っている

☐ **content** 形 満足している

☐ **contest** 動 反論する, 争う

☐ **control** 動 抑制する, コントロールする

☐ **convent** 名 女子修道院

☐ **conversation** 名 会話, 会談

☐ **convict** 名 罪人, 囚人

☐ **convince** 動 納得させる, 確信させる

☐ **corpse** 名 (人間の) 死体, 死骸

☐ **Cosette** 名 コゼット《人名》

☐ **could** 熟 How could 〜? 何だって〜なんてことがありえようか？ If +《主語》+ could 〜できればなあ《仮定法》could have done 〜だったかもしれない《仮定法》

☐ **count** 名 計算, 総計, 勘定 on all counts あらゆる面 [点] で

☐ **couple** 名 ①2つ, 対 ②夫婦, 一組

☐ **coupled** 形 結合した, 連結した coupled with 〜と相まって, 〜を加味して

☐ **courage** 名 勇気, 度胸

☐ **Courfeyrac** 名 クールフェラック《人名》

☐ **course** 熟 of course もちろん, 当

然
- □ **courthouse** 名 裁判所
- □ **cover** 動 覆う, 包む, 隠す
- □ **crash** 名 (壊れるときの)すさまじい音
- □ **crawl** 動 はう, 腹ばいで進む, ゆっくり進む
- □ **creep** 動 のろのろ進む, ゆっくり動く creep up ジリジリと上がる[増大する]
- □ **crepe** 名 クレープ織りの喪章
- □ **crept** 動 creep (ゆっくり動く)の過去, 過去分詞
- □ **crest** 動 頂点に達する
- □ **crime** 名 ①(法律上の)罪, 犯罪 ②悪事, よくない行為
- □ **criminal** 名 犯罪者, 犯人
- □ **crooked** 形 湾曲した, 曲がった
- □ **cross over** (領域・枠などを)越える
- □ **crowd** 名 群集, 雑踏, 多数, 聴衆
- □ **cruel** 形 残酷な, 厳しい
- □ **crumble** 動 ～を砕く, 粉々になる[する] crumble away 砕け散る, 消え失せる
- □ **cry out** 叫ぶ
- □ **cunning** 名 狡猾さ, ずるさ
- □ **cupboard** 名 食器棚, 戸棚
- □ **curiosity** 名 ①好奇心 ②珍しい物[存在]
- □ **curious** 形 好奇心の強い, 珍しい, 奇妙な, 知りたがる
- □ **currently** 副 今のところ, 現在
- □ **cut off** 切断する, 切り離す

D

- □ **daily** 形 毎日の, 日常の
- □ **damage** 名 損害, 損傷
- □ **darken** 動 暗くする[なる]
- □ **darkness** 名 暗さ, 暗やみ
- □ **dart** 動 (矢, 視線などを)投げる, 射る
- □ **day** 熟 day and night 昼も夜も each day 毎日, 日ごとに good day こんにちは one day (過去の)ある日, (未来の)いつか one of these days いずれそのうちに, 近日中に these days このごろ
- □ **daytime** 名 昼間
- □ **deal** 動 ①分配する ②《 – with [in] ～》～を扱う
- □ **dearly** 副 とても, 心から
- □ **death** 名 死, 死ぬこと
- □ **deceive** 動 だます, あざむく
- □ **declare** 動 宣言する
- □ **deed** 名 行為, 行動
- □ **deeply** 副 深く, 非常に
- □ **deliver** 動 配達する, 伝える
- □ **demand** 動 要求する, 尋ねる
- □ **denounce** 動 非難する, 告発する
- □ **despair** 名 絶望, 自暴自棄
- □ **desperate** 形 ①絶望的な, 見込みのない ②ほしくてたまらない, 必死の
- □ **desperation** 名 自暴自棄, やけ, 絶望
- □ **despise** 動 軽蔑する
- □ **despite** 前 ～にもかかわらず
- □ **destiny** 名 運命, 宿命
- □ **detail** 名 細部, 《-s》詳細
- □ **devastate** 動 荒らす, 荒廃させる,

困惑させる

- ☐ **develop** 動 ①発達する［させる］②開発する
- ☐ **die of** 〜がもとで死ぬ
- ☐ **dignity** 名 威厳, 品位, 尊さ, 敬意
- ☐ **dim** 形 薄暗い, 見にくい
- ☐ **direct** 形 まっすぐな, 直接の, 率直な
- ☐ **dirty** 形 汚い, 汚れた
- ☐ **disappear** 動 見えなくなる, 姿を消す, なくなる
- ☐ **disappoint** 動 失望させる, がっかりさせる
- ☐ **discovery** 名 発見
- ☐ **disinherit** 動 〜から相続権を奪う
- ☐ **dismay** 名 ろうばい, 落胆, 幻滅
- ☐ **dismiss** 動 解雇する
- ☐ **dismissal** 名 解放, 放免, 解雇
- ☐ **display** 動 展示する, 示す
- ☐ **distance** 名 距離, 隔たり, 遠方 in the distance 遠方に
- ☐ **distant** 形 ①遠い, 隔たった ②よそよそしい, 距離のある
- ☐ **disturb** 動 かき乱す, 妨げる
- ☐ **do harm** 害を及ぼす, ためにならない
- ☐ **do with** 〜を処理する
- ☐ **door** 熟 knock on the door ドアをノックする
- ☐ **doorway** 名 戸口, 玄関, 出入り口
- ☐ **doubtless** 副 疑いなく, 確かに, おそらく
- ☐ **down** 熟 come down 下りて来る lie down 横たわる, 横になる look down 見下ろす look down at 〜に目［視線］を落とす put down 下に置く, 下ろす roll down 転がり落ちる

turn down 曲がって〜へ行く

- ☐ **downcast** 形 うつむいた, 意気消沈した
- ☐ **dozen** 名 1ダース, 12（個）
- ☐ **drag** 動 ①引きずる ②のろのろ動く［動かす］ drag out 引きずり出す
- ☐ **dreamy** 形 夢を見る, 空想にふける
- ☐ **driver** 名（馬車の）御者
- ☐ **dumbfounded** 形 あぜんとした, びっくりした
- ☐ **dust** 動 ①ちり［ほこり］を払う ②（〜に…を）まぶす
- ☐ **duty** 名 義務（感）, 責任
- ☐ **dying** 形 死にかかっている, 消えそうな

E

- ☐ **each day** 毎日, 日ごとに
- ☐ **each other** お互いに
- ☐ **eager** 形 ①熱心な ②《be – for 〜》〜を切望している,《be – to 〜》しきりに〜したがっている
- ☐ **earn** 動 ①儲ける, 稼ぐ ②（名声を）博す
- ☐ **earnings** 名 所得, 収入, 稼ぎ
- ☐ **easily** 副 ①容易に, たやすく, 苦もなく ②気楽に
- ☐ **edge** 名 ①刃 ②端, 縁
- ☐ **education** 名 教育, 教養
- ☐ **effort** 名 努力（の成果）
- ☐ **either A or B** Aかそれともв
- ☐ **elder** 形 年上の, 年長の
- ☐ **elegant** 形 上品な, 優雅な
- ☐ **element** 名 要素, 成分, 元素
- ☐ **embrace** 動 抱き締める

☐ **emperor** 名皇帝, 天皇

☐ **employ** 動(人を)雇う, 使う

☐ **employee** 名従業員, 会社員, 被雇用者

☐ **employer** 名雇主, 使用[利用]する人

☐ **end** 熟 in the end とうとう, 結局, ついに

☐ **engagement** 名婚約, 約束

☐ **England** 名①イングランド ②英国

☐ **Enjolras** 名アンジョルラス《人名》

☐ **enough to do** ～するのに十分な

☐ **enroll** 動登録する, 入会する, 入学する

☐ **entire** 形全体の, 完全な, まったくの

☐ **entirely** 副完全に, まったく

☐ **entrust** 動ゆだねる, 任せる, 委託する

☐ **Eponine** 名エポニーヌ《人名》

☐ **equal** 名同等のもの[人]

☐ **escape** 動逃げる, 免れる, もれる 名逃亡, 脱出, もれ

☐ **establish** 動確立する, 立証する, 設置[設立]する

☐ **even better** さらに素晴らしいことに

☐ **eventually** 副結局は

☐ **ever since** それ以来ずっと

☐ **everybody** 代誰でも, 皆

☐ **everyday** 形毎日の, 日々の

☐ **everyone** 代誰でも, 皆

☐ **everything** 代すべてのこと[もの], 何でも, 何もかも everything but ～ 以外のすべてのこと[もの]

☐ **evict** 動～を強制退去させる

☐ **evidence** 名証拠

☐ **ex-convict** 名前科者

☐ **exact** 形正確な, 厳密な, きちょうめんな

☐ **except** 前～を除いて, ～のほかは

☐ **exclaim** 動①(喜び・驚きなどで)声をあげる ②声高に激しく言う

☐ **exclamation** 名(喜び・驚きなどの)叫び, 感嘆

☐ **exile** 動追放する

☐ **expense** 名出費, 費用

☐ **explosion** 名爆発, 急増

☐ **expose** 動①さらす, 露出する ②(秘密などを)暴露する

☐ **express** 動表現する, 述べる

☐ **extreme** 形極端な, 極度の, いちばん端の

F

☐ **fact** 熟 in fact つまり, 実は, 要するに

☐ **factory** 名工場, 製造所

☐ **fade** 動消えていく, 薄くなる, 衰える fade away 消えていく

☐ **fail** 動失敗する

☐ **faint** 名気絶, 失神 feel faint 気絶しそうだ

☐ **fair** 形正しい, 公平[正当]な

☐ **fake** 形にせの

☐ **fall back** 後退する, 戻る, 退却する

☐ **fall in love with** 恋におちる

☐ **fall on** ～に降りかかる

☐ **fall over** ～につまずく, ～の上に倒れかかる

A
B
C
D
E
F
G
H
I
J
K
L
M
N
O
P
Q
R
S
T
U
V
W
X
Y
Z

☐ **fall to one's knee** くずれ落ちて ひざをつく

☐ **fallen** 動 fall (落ちる) の過去分詞

☐ **falling** 形 落下する, 転落する

☐ **falter** 動 ためらう, くじける

☐ **familiar with** 《be – 》~をよく 知っている, ~と親しい

☐ **fancy** 動 ①心に描く, (~と) 考える ②好む, 引かれる

☐ **Fantine** 名 ファンティーヌ《人名》

☐ **far from** ~から遠い, ~どころか

☐ **fate** 名 運命, 宿命

☐ **fateful** 形 運命を決める, 致命的な

☐ **Fauchelevent** 名 フォーシュルヴ ァン《人名》

☐ **fault** 名 過失, 誤り

☐ **fear** 名 ①恐れ ②心配, 不安 動 ①恐れる ②心配する

☐ **fed** 動 feed (供給する) の過去, 過去 分詞

☐ **feed** 動 ①食物を与える ②供給する feed into ~に流れ込む

☐ **feel a presence** 気配を感じる

☐ **feel faint** 気絶しそうだ

☐ **feel like** ~がほしい, ~したい気が する, ~のような感じがする

☐ **feet** 熟 on one's feet 立っている状 態で put ~ back on its feet ~を 再建する

☐ **fight off** 戦って撃退する

☐ **fighting** 名 戦闘

☐ **figure** 名 人 [物] の姿, 形 動 ①描 写する, 想像する ②計算する ③目立 つ, (~として) 現れる figure out 理 解する, ~であるとわかる, (原因など を) 解明する

☐ **filled with** 《be – 》~でいっぱい になる

☐ **filth** 名 ごみ, 汚物

☐ **filthy** 形 汚い, 汚れた, 下品な, みだ らな

☐ **financial** 形 財務(上) の, 金融(上) の

☐ **find out** 見つけ出す, 気がつく, 知る, 調べる, 解明する

☐ **firmly** 副 しっかりと, 断固として

☐ **first** 熟 at first 最初は, 初めのうち は

☐ **fit** 動 合致 [適合] する, 合致させる 名 適合, 一致, 調和

☐ **flash** 名 閃光, きらめき

☐ **fled** 動 flee (逃げる) の過去, 過去分 詞

☐ **fling** 動 ~を放り投げる

☐ **flung** 動 fling (投げつける) の過去, 過去分詞

☐ **flutter** 動 (脈, 心臓が) 激しく不規 則に打つ, そわそわする

☐ **fold** 動 折りたたむ, 包む

☐ **folk song** 民謡

☐ **following** 形 次に続く

☐ **fool** 名 ばか者, おろかな人

☐ **foolish** 形 おろかな, ばかばかしい

☐ **footstep** 名 足音, 歩み

☐ **for all ~** ~にもかかわらず

☐ **for long** 長い間

☐ **for nothing** ただで, 無料で, むだ に

☐ **for some time** しばらくの間

☐ **force** 名 力, 勢い 動 ①強制する, 力 ずくで~する, 余儀なく~させる ②押 しやる, 押し込む

☐ **forehead** 名 ひたい

□ **forgive** 動許す, 免除する

□ **forgiven** 動forgive (許す) の過去分詞

□ **former** 形前の, 先の, 以前の

□ **fortune** 名富, 財産

□ **forward** 副①前方に ②将来に向けて ③先へ, 進んで

□ **franc** 名フラン《貨幣》

□ **France** 名フランス《国名》

□ **frantically** 副取り乱して, 半狂乱で

□ **frayed** 形 (布などが) 擦り切れた

□ **French** 形フランス (人・語) の 名①フランス語 ②《the – 》フランス人

□ **frequent** 形ひんばんな, よくある

□ **fried** 形油で揚げた, フライ料理の

□ **frightened** 形おびえた, びっくりした

□ **front** 熟in front of ～の前に, ～の正面に

□ **frustration** 名欲求不満, 失意, 挫折

□ **fulfill** 動 (義務・約束を) 果たす, (要求・条件を) 満たす

□ **fully** 副十分に, 完全に, まるまる

□ **fun** 熟have fun 楽しむ

□ **furniture** 名家具, 備品, 調度

□ **fury** 名激しい怒り

G

□ **gain** 動得る, 増す

□ **galley** 名ガレー船《古代から中世にかけて使われたオールと帆で進む大型船》galley slave ガレー船を漕ぐ奴隷

□ **gardener** 名庭師, 園芸家

□ **gather** 動①集まる, 集める ②生じる, 増す

□ **Gavroche** 名ガヴローシュ《人名》

□ **general** 熟in general 一般に, たいてい

□ **generosity** 名①寛大, 気前のよさ ②豊富さ

□ **generous** 形①寛大な, 気前のよい ②豊富な

□ **get** 熟get a job 職を得る get close to ～に近づく, 接近する get into bed ベッドに入る get off (～から) 降りる get out of bed 起きる, 寝床を離れる get through 乗り切る, ～を通り抜ける get to (事) を始める, ～に達する [到着する]

□ **gift** 名贈り物

□ **Gillenormand** 名ジルノルマン《人名》

□ **give away** ただで与える, 贈る, 譲歩する, 手放す

□ **give up** あきらめる, やめる, 引き渡す

□ **glad to** 《be – 》～してうれしい, 喜んで～する

□ **glance** 名ちらっと見ること, 一べつ

□ **glare** 動にらみつける

□ **gleam** 動キラリと光る

□ **glimpse** 名ちらりと見ること catch a glimpse of ～をちらっと見る, 垣間見る

□ **go** 熟go around 動き回る, あちらこちらに行く, 回り道をする go away 立ち去る go back to ～に帰る [戻る], ～に遡る, (中断していた作業に) 再び取り掛かる go by ～に基づいて [よって] 行う go by the name of 通称～

A
B
C
D
E
F
G
H
I
J
K
L
M
N
O
P
Q
R
S
T
U
V
W
X
Y
Z

と呼ばれている **go for a walk** 散歩に行く **go into** 〜に入る，（仕事）に就く **go off** 爆発する，発射する **go on** 続く，続ける，進み続ける，起こる，発生する **go out** 外出する，外へ出る **go shopping** 買い物に行く **go through** 通り抜ける，一つずつ順番に検討する **go up** ①〜に上がる，登る ②〜に近づく，出かける ③（建物などが）建つ，立つ **go up to** 〜まで行く，近づく

☐ **God** 名神，創造主 間 やれやれ，何てことだ **My God.** おや，まあ

☐ **good** 熟 **be good at** 〜が得意だ **be not good for** 〜に良くない **good day** こんにちは **take good care of** 〜を大事に扱う，大切にする

☐ **goodness** 名善良さ，よいところ 間 何てことだ！，大変だ！

☐ **government** 名政治，政府，支配

☐ **grab** 動ふいにつかむ

☐ **gradually** 副だんだんと

☐ **graduation** 名卒業（式）

☐ **grand** 形雄大な，壮麗な

☐ **grandson** 名孫息子

☐ **grass** 名草，芝生

☐ **grate** 名鉄格子

☐ **grateful** 形感謝する，ありがたく思う

☐ **gratefully** 副感謝して，ありがたく

☐ **gratitude** 名感謝（の気持ち），報恩の念

☐ **grave** 名墓

☐ **greatly** 副大いに

☐ **grim** 形 ①（表情などが）険しい，こわい ②厳しい，残酷な

☐ **grimly** 副残忍に，険しい顔で

☐ **grow up** 成長する，大人になる

☐ **guardian** 名保護者，守護神

☐ **guest** 名客，ゲスト

☐ **guilt** 名罪，有罪，犯罪

☐ **guilty** 形有罪の，やましい

☐ **gun** 名銃，大砲

☐ **gunpowder** 名火薬

H

☐ **habit** 名習慣，癖，気質 **be in the habit of 〜ing** 〜する習慣がある

☐ **halfway** 副中間［中途］で 形中間［中途］の

☐ **hall** 名公会堂，ホール，大広間，玄関

☐ **hand** 熟 **hand over hand**（ロープなどを）両手でたぐって **on the other hand** 一方，他方では

☐ **handful** 名一握り，少量

☐ **handle** 動操縦する，取り扱う

☐ **handsome** 形端正な（顔立ちの），りっぱな，（男性が）ハンサムな

☐ **hang** 動かかる，かける，つるす，ぶら下がる **hang on** 〜につかまる，〜に掛けられる

☐ **happen to** たまたま〜する，偶然〜する

☐ **happily** 副幸福に，楽しく，うまく，幸いにも

☐ **happiness** 名幸せ，喜び

☐ **hard time** 《a－》つらい時期

☐ **hard to** 〜し難い

☐ **hardened** 形冷淡な，かたくなな

☐ **harm** 動傷つける，損なう 名害，損害 **do harm** 害を及ぼす，ためにならない

☐ **have** 熟 could have done ～だったかもしれない《仮定法》 have fun 楽しむ have no idea わからない have nothing left to live for 生きがいが何もない

☐ **head of** ～の長

☐ **headquarters** 名本部, 司令部, 本署

☐ **healthy** 形健康な, 健全な, 健康によい

☐ **hear from** ～から手紙［電話・返事］をもらう

☐ **heartbroken** 形悲しみに打ちひしがれた

☐ **heaven** 名天国

☐ **heed** 名注意

☐ **here** 熟 here and there あちこちで here are ～ こちらは～です。 Look here. ほら。ねえ。

☐ **hid** 動 hide (隠れる) の過去, 過去分詞

☐ **hidden** 形隠れた, 秘密の

☐ **hide** 動隠れる, 隠す, 隠れて見えない, 秘密にする

☐ **hiding** 名隠す［隠れる］こと

☐ **hired** 形雇われた

☐ **hold on** しっかりつかまる

☐ **hold up** 維持する, 支える

☐ **home** 熟 bring home 家に持ってくる take someone home (人) を家まで送る

☐ **hometown** 名①生まれ故郷, 出身地 ②現在住んでいる町

☐ **honest** 形①正直な, 誠実な, 心からの ②公正な, 感心な

☐ **horrible** 形恐ろしい, ひどい

☐ **horror** 名①恐怖, ぞっとすること

②嫌悪

☐ **hostile** 形敵意をもった, 敵の

☐ **How could ～?** 何だって～なんてことがありえようか?

☐ **how to** ～する方法

☐ **however** 接けれども, だが

☐ **hundred-franc note** 100フラン紙幣

☐ **hundreds of** 何百もの～

☐ **hunt** 動狩る, 狩りをする, 探し求める

☐ **hunting** 名狩り, 狩猟, ハンティング

☐ **hurry** 熟 in a hurry 急いで, あわてて

☐ **hush** 間しっ! 静かに!

I

☐ **icy** 形氷の (多い), 氷のように冷たい

☐ **idea** 熟 have no idea わからない

☐ **identity** 名①同一であること ②本人であること

☐ **if** 熟 If ＋《主語》＋ could ～できればなあ《仮定法》 as if あたかも～のように, まるで～みたいに ask ～ if ～かどうか尋ねる wonder if ～ではないかと思う

☐ **ignore** 動無視する, 怠る

☐ **immediate** 形さっそくの, 即座の, 直接の

☐ **immediately** 副すぐに, ～するやいなや

☐ **immense** 形巨大な, 計り知れない, すばらしい

☐ **importantly** 副重大に, もったいぶって

A
B
C
D
E
F
G
H
I
J
K
L
M
N
O
P
Q
R
S
T
U
V
W
X
Y
Z

- □ **imposter** 名なりすまし, 偽物
- □ **imprisonment** 名投獄, 交流
- □ **in** 熟 in time 間に合って just in time いよいよというときに, ぎりぎりセーフで
- □ **including** 前 ～を含めて, 込みで
- □ **income** 名収入, 所得, 収益
- □ **indeed** 副①実際, 本当に ②《強意》まったく 間本当に, まさか
- □ **influence** 名影響, 勢力
- □ **inherit** 動相続する, 受け継ぐ
- □ **inheritance** 名相続(財産), 遺産
- □ **inn** 名宿屋
- □ **innkeeper** 名宿屋の主人[経営者]
- □ **innocent** 形無実の
- □ **inquire** 動尋ねる, 調べる, 調査する inquire into ～の取り調べをする
- □ **insist** 動①主張する, 断言する ②要求する
- □ **inspector** 名警部補
- □ **instead** 副その代わりに instead of ～の代わりに, ～をしないで
- □ **instinctually** 副本能的に, 直感的に
- □ **intent** 名意図, 意向
- □ **interior** 形内部の
- □ **interrupt** 動さえぎる, 妨害する, 口をはさむ
- □ **invent** 動発明[考案]する
- □ **invention** 名発明(品)
- □ **inventive** 形発明の, 発明の才のある, 創意に富む
- □ **invitation** 名招待(状), 案内(状)
- □ **involve** 動①含む, 伴う ②巻き込む, かかわらせる
- □ **iron** 形鉄の, 鉄製の

- □ **isolated** 形隔離した, 孤立した
- □ **It is ～ for someone to ...** (人)が…するのは～だ

J

- □ **jail** 名刑務所 動拘置する, 投獄する
- □ **Javert** 名ジャベール《人名》
- □ **jealous** 形嫉妬して, 嫉妬深い, うらやんで
- □ **Jean Valjean** ジャン・ヴァルジャン《人名》
- □ **job** 熟 get a job 職を得る
- □ **journey** 名①(遠い目的地への)旅 ②行程
- □ **joy** 名喜び, 楽しみ
- □ **judge** 名裁判官, 判事
- □ **just as** (ちょうど)であろうとおり
- □ **just in time** いよいよというときに, すんでのところで, やっと間に合って
- □ **just then** そのとたんに

K

- □ **keep one's promise** 約束を守る
- □ **keep someone from** ～から(人)を阻む
- □ **keg** 名小さなたる
- □ **kind of** ある程度, いくらか, ～のようなもの[人]
- □ **kind-looking** 形親切そうな
- □ **kindness** 名親切(な行為), 優しさ
- □ **kiss** 動キスする
- □ **knee** 名ひざ
- □ **kneel** 動ひざまずく, ひざをつく

fall to one's knee くずれ落ちてひざ
をつく kneel down ひざまずく, ひざ
をつく

☐ **knife** 名ナイフ, 小刀, 包丁, 短剣

☐ **knock** 動ノックする, たたく, ぶつ
ける knock on the door ドアをノッ
クする 名打つこと, 戸をたたくこと
［音］

☐ **know of** ～について知っている

L

☐ **laid** 動 lay（置く）の過去, 過去分詞

☐ **lamp** 名ランプ, 灯火

☐ **landing** 名（階段の）踊り場

☐ **landlady** 名女家主, 女主人

☐ **landlord** 名（男の）家主, 地主

☐ **lantern** 名手提げランプ, ランタン

☐ **largely** 副大いに, 主として

☐ **lay** 動 lie（横たわる）の過去

☐ **lead the way** 先に立って導く, 案
内する, 率先する

☐ **leave** 熟 have nothing left to live
for 生きがいが何もない leave ～
alone ～をそっとしておく

☐ **led** 動 lead（導く）の過去, 過去分詞

☐ **legal** 形法律（上）の, 正当な

☐ **Les Misérables** レ・ミゼラブル
《惨めな人々という意味のフランス語》

☐ **less** 副 ～より少なく, ～ほどでなく
much less まして～でない

☐ **let us** どうか私たちに～させてくだ
さい

☐ **level** 名水準

☐ **lie** 動 ①うそをつく ②横たわる, 寝
る ③（ある状態に）ある, 存在する lie
down 横たわる, 横になる 名うそ

☐ **life** 熟 all one's life ずっと, 生まれ
てから come to life 目覚める, 復活
する

☐ **lift** 動 ①持ち上げる, 上がる ②取り
除く, 撤廃する

☐ **light up** 晴れやかになる, 明るい顔
になる

☐ **like** 熟 Would you like ～? ～は
いかがですか。 feel like ～がほし
い, ～したい気がする, ～のような感じ
がする like this このような, こんなふ
うに look like ～のように見える, ～
に似ている rather like ～に似ている
would like to ～したいと思う

☐ **limply** 副ぐにゃっとして

☐ **lining** 名裏地

☐ **list** 動名簿［目録］に記入する, リス
トアップする

☐ **lit** 動 light（火をつける）の過去, 過去
分詞

☐ **live** 熟 have nothing left to live
for 生きがいが何もない

☐ **load** 動（銃弾を銃に）装填する, 込め
る

☐ **loaf** 名パンひとかたまり loaf of《a
－》ひとかたまりの～

☐ **lodging** 名宿泊, 宿

☐ **London** 名ロンドン《英国の首都》

☐ **lonely** 形 ①孤独な, 心さびしい
②ひっそりした, 人里離れた

☐ **long** 熟 as long as ～する以上は,
～である限りは for long 長い間 no
longer もはや～でない［～しない］
not ～ any longer もはや～でない［～
しない］

☐ **look** 熟 look after ～の世話をす
る, ～に気をつける look around ま
わりを見回す look back at ～に視

A
B
C
D
E
F
G
H
I
J
K
L
M
N
O
P
Q
R
S
T
U
V
W
X
Y
Z

線を戻す, ～を振り返って見る look down 見下ろす look down at ～に目[視線]を落とす look for ～を探す Look here. ほら。ねえ。 look into ①～を検討する, ～を研究する ②～の中を見る, ～をのぞき込む look like ～のように見える, ～に似ている look on 傍観する, 眺める look out ①外を見る ②気をつける, 注意する look through ～をのぞき込む look up 見上げる, 調べる look up to ～を仰ぎ見る

□ **loud** 熟 out loud 言いたいことを大きな声で, 公然と wonder out loud 疑い[疑問]を口に出す

□ **love** 熟 be in love with ～に恋して, ～に心を奪われて fall in love with 恋におちる love affair 恋愛

□ **lover** 名 愛人, 恋人

□ **lower** 動 下げる, 低くする

□ **luckily** 副 運よく, 幸いにも

□ **luis** 名 ルイ金貨

□ **Luxembourg** 名 リュクサンブール宮殿《広大な庭園が付随し公園となっている》

□ **lying** 動 lie (横たわる)の現在分詞

M

□ **Madeleine** 名 マドレーヌ《人名》

□ **Mademoiselle** 名 ～嬢, 令嬢, マドモアゼル

□ **maid** 名 お手伝い, メイド

□ **main** 形 主な, 主要な

□ **make one's way** 進む, 行く

□ **make out** 作り上げる, 認識する, 見分ける

□ **make up** 作り出す, 考え出す, ～を構成[形成]する

□ **manner** 名 ①方法, やり方 ②態度, 様子 ③《-s》行儀, 作法, 生活様式

□ **mantle** 名 暖炉の飾り棚

□ **manufacture** 名 製造, 製作, 製品

□ **many** 熟 so many 非常に多くの

□ **Marius** 名 マリウス《人名》

□ **mark** 動 ①印[記号]をつける ②目立たせる

□ **marking** 名 ①印をつけること ②印, 斑点

□ **marriage** 名 結婚(生活・式)

□ **married** 動 marry (結婚する)の過去, 過去分詞 形 結婚した, 既婚の

□ **marry** 動 結婚する

□ **matter** 熟 no matter ～を問わず, どうでもいい matter to ～にとって大切である

□ **May I ～?** ～してもよいですか。

□ **mayor** 名 市長

□ **meantime** 名 合間, その間 in the meantime それまでは, 当分は

□ **meanwhile** 副 それまでの間, 一方では

□ **meditation** 名 瞑想, 黙想

□ **meeting** 名 集まり, ミーティング

□ **mend** 動 直す, 繕う

□ **mention** 動 (～について)述べる, 言及する

□ **mere** 形 単なる, ほんの, まったく～にすぎない

□ **middle** 名 中間, 最中 in the middle of ～の真ん中[中ほど]に

□ **midst** 名 真ん中, 中央

□ **might** 名 力

□ **mind** 名 ①心, 精神, 考え ②知性

動 ①気にする, いやがる ②気をつける, 用心する

□ **mirror** 名鏡

□ **miserable** 形 みじめな, 哀れな

□ **misery** 名 ①悲惨, みじめさ ②苦痛, 不幸, 苦難

□ **mistaken** 形 誤った

□ **mistakenly** 副 間違って, 誤解して

□ **mistreatment** 名 酷使, 虐待

□ **misunderstanding** 名 考え違い, 誤解

□ **moment** 名 ①瞬間, ちょっとの間 ②(特定の) 時, 時期 at the moment 今は for a moment 少しの間 in a moment ただちに one moment ちょっとの間

□ **Monsieur** 名 ~氏《フランス語で Mr./Sir にあたる敬称》

□ **monster** 名 怪物

□ **Montfermeil** 名 モンフェルメイユ《地名》

□ **Montpercy** 名 モンペルシー《人名》

□ **Montreuil-sur-Mer** 名 モントルイユ・シュル・メール《地名》

□ **mood** 名 気分, 機嫌, 雰囲気, 憂うつ

□ **moonlight** 名 月明かり, 月光

□ **more** 熟 more and more ますます more than ~以上 no more もう~ない

□ **morning** 熟 one morning ある朝

□ **moss** 名 コケ《植物》

□ **Mother Superir** 女子修道院長

□ **motion** 名 身振り, 動作 動 身振りで合図する

□ **mourning** 名 ①悲嘆, 哀悼 ②服喪, 哀悼の意を表すこと

□ **move away from** ~から遠ざかる

□ **move to** ~に引っ越す

□ **much less** まして~でない

□ **murder** 名 人殺し, 殺害, 殺人事件

□ **murderer** 名 殺人犯

□ **musket** 名 マスケット銃

□ **muzzle** 名 銃口

□ **My God.** おや, まあ

□ **mysterious** 形 神秘的な, 謎めいた

N

□ **name** 熟 go by the name of 通称 ~と呼ばれている

□ **Napoleon Bonaparte** ナポレオン・ボナパルト《フランスの軍人, 政治家。1769-1821》

□ **narrow** 形 ①狭い ②限られた 動 狭くなる[する]

□ **nearby** 形 近くの, 間近の

□ **necessary** 形 必要な, 必然の

□ **neglect** 動 ①無視する, 怠る ②放置する, 軽視する

□ **neighborhood** 名 近所(の人々), 付近

□ **neither** 形 どちらの~も…でない 代 (2者のうち) どちらも~でない 副《否定文に続いて》 ~も…しない neither ~ nor … ~も…もない

□ **nervous** 形 ①神経の ②神経質な, おどおどした

□ **nest** 名 巣

□ **nestle** 動 快適な場所に落ち着く, (~を)心地よく落ち着かせる nestle into (建物などが) ~に佇む

□ **news** 名 報道, ニュース, 便り, 知ら

A B C D E F G H I J K L M N O P Q R S T U V W X Y Z

せ

- **newspaper** 名 新聞（紙）
- **next to** ～のとなりに，～の次に
- **night** 熟 day and night 昼も夜も the night before 前の晩
- **no** 熟 have no idea わからない no longer もはや～でない［～しない］ no matter ～を問わず，どうでもいい no more もう～ない no one 誰も［一人も］ ～ない there is no way ～する見込みはない
- **noble** 形 気高い，高貴な
- **nobody** 代 誰も［1人も］～ない
- **nod** 動 うなずく
- **nor** 接 ～もまたない Nor do I.《否定の文に続けて》私も（いや）です。 neither ～ nor … ～も…もない
- **normal** 形 普通の，平均の，標準的な
- **not** 熟 be not good for ～に良くない not ～ any longer もはや～でない［～しない］ not ～ but … ～ではなくて…
- **note** 名 メモ，覚え書き
- **notebook** 名 ノート，手帳
- **nothing** 熟 all for nothing むだに have nothing left to live for 生きがいが何もない
- **notice** 動 気づく，認める
- **now** 熟 for now 今のところ，ひとまず now that 今や～だから，～からには right now 今すぐに，たった今
- **numb** 形 しびれた，麻痺した，感覚のない
- **numerous** 形 多数の
- **nun** 名 修道女，尼僧

O

- **oblivious** 形 忘れている，気にしない
- **occasion** 名 ①場合，(特定の)時 ②機会，好機 ③理由，根拠
- **occupation** 名 職業，仕事，就業
- **of course** もちろん，当然
- **of which** ～の中で
- **off** 熟 cut off 切断する，切り離す fight off 戦って撃退する get off (～から)降りる go off 爆発する，発射する run off into ～の中に逃げ込む take off (衣服を)脱ぐ，取り去る walk off 立ち去る
- **offer** 動 申し出る，申し込む，提供する
- **officer** 名 役人，公務員，警察官 police officer 警察官
- **on all counts** あらゆる面［点］で
- **on one's feet** 立っている状態で
- **on the other hand** 一方，他方では
- **on top of** ～の上（部）に
- **one** 熟 no one 誰も［一人も］～ない one day (過去の)ある日，(未来の)いつか one moment ちょっとの間 one morning ある朝 one of these days いずれそのうちに，近日中に
- **onto** 前 ～の上へ［に］
- **open** 熟 break open (金庫などを)こじ開ける
- **option** 名 選択（の余地），選択可能物，選択権
- **or so** ～かそこらで
- **ordinary** 形 ①普通の，通常の ②並の，平凡な

□ **other** 熟 each other お互いに on the other hand 一方, 他方では

□ **out loud** 言いたいことを大きな声で, 公然と wonder out loud 疑い[疑問]を口に出す

□ **out of** ①～から外へ, ～から抜け出して ②～から作り出して, ～を材料として ③～の範囲外に, ～から離れて ④(ある数)の中から

□ **outburst** 名 爆発, 噴出

□ **over** 熟 climb over ～を乗り越える come over やって来る, ～の身にふりかかる cross over (領域・枠などを)越える fall over ～につまずく, ～の上に倒れかかる hand over hand (ロープなどを)両手でたぐって watch over 見守る, 見張る

□ **overheard** 動 overhear (ふと耳にする)の過去, 過去分詞

□ **overjoyed** 形 大喜びの

□ **overnight** 副 一晩中, 夜通し

□ **overtaken** 動 overtake (追いつく)の過去分詞

□ **overwhelm** 動 力で圧倒する, 苦しむ, 混乱する

□ **owe** 動 ①(～を)負う, (～を人の)お陰とする ②(金を)借りている, (人に対して～の)義務がある

P

□ **pack** 動 荷造りする, 詰め込む

□ **package** 名 包み, 小包, パッケージ

□ **paid** 動 pay (払う)の過去, 過去分詞

□ **pair** 名 (2つから成る)一対, 一組, ペア

□ **pale** 形 (顔色・人が)青ざめた, 青白い

□ **pang** 名 発作, 激痛, 心の痛み

□ **panic** 名 パニック, 恐慌

□ **paperwork** 名 書類仕事

□ **parade** 動 行進する parade around うろつく

□ **parent** 名《-s》両親

□ **Paris** 名 パリ《フランスの首都》

□ **particular** 形 特定の

□ **particularly** 副 特に, とりわけ

□ **pass away** 死ぬ

□ **pass through** ～を通る, 通行する

□ **passion** 名 情熱, (～への)熱中, 激怒

□ **passionately** 副 激しく, 猛烈に

□ **past** 形 過去の, この前の 名 過去(の出来事) 前《時間・場所》～を過ぎて, ～を越して walk past 通り過ぎる

□ **pause** 名 (活動の)中止, 休止 動 休止する, 立ち止まる

□ **pay** 動 支払う, 払う pay a visit ～を訪問する

□ **peace** 熟 in peace 平和のうちに, 安心して

□ **peer** 動 じっと見る

□ **pension** 名 年金, 恩給

□ **Peré Lachaise** ペール・ラシェーズ《地名, パリ最大の墓地》

□ **perhaps** 副 たぶん, ことによると

□ **permission** 名 許可, 免許

□ **pertain** 動 関係する

□ **philanthropist** 名 慈善家

□ **philosophical** 形 哲学の, 理性的な, 賢明な

□ **philosophy** 名 哲学, 主義, 信条,

A B C D E F G H I J K L M N O P Q R S T U V W X Y Z

人生観

- **pick up** 拾い上げる, 車で迎えに行く, 習得する, 再開する, 回復する
- **pile** 名 積み重ね, (～の)山
- **pillar** 名 柱, 支柱
- **pistol** 名 拳銃
- **pity** 名 哀れみ, 同情, 残念なこと 動 気の毒に思う, 哀れむ
- **plaster** 名 しっくい, 壁土, 石膏
- **plate** 名 (浅い)皿
- **platoon** 名 小隊
- **play with** ～で遊ぶ, ～と一緒に遊ぶ
- **plead** 動 嘆願する, 訴える
- **pleased** 形 喜んだ, 気に入った
- **pleasure** 名 喜び, 楽しみ, 満足, 娯楽
- **plenty** 名 十分, たくさん, 豊富 plenty of たくさんの～
- **plus** 前 ～を加えて
- **point** 熟 to the point 要領を得た
- **police officer** 警察官
- **policeman** 名 警察官
- **policemen** 名 policeman(警察官)の複数
- **political** 形 ①政治の, 政党の ②策略的な
- **politics** 名 政治(学), 政策
- **ponder** 動 じっくり考える, 熟考する
- **Pontmarie** 名 ポンマリー《人名》
- **Pontmercy** 名 ポンメルシー《人名》
- **portrait** 名 肖像画
- **pose** 動 見せかける
- **position** 名 地位, 身分, 職
- **possibly** 副《否定文, 疑問文で》どうしても, できる限り, とても, なんとか

- **pour** 動 注ぐ, 浴びせる
- **powder** 名 粉末, おしろい, 火薬
- **powerful-looking** 形 力強そうな
- **pray** 動 祈る
- **prayer** 名 祈り, 祈願(文)
- **prefer** 動 (～のほうを)好む, (～のほうが)よいと思う
- **preparation** 名 ①準備, したく ②心構え
- **prepare for** ～の準備をする
- **presence** 名 ①存在すること ②出席, 態度 feel a presence 気配を感じる
- **pretend** 動 ①ふりをする, 装う ②あえて～しようとする
- **prey** 名 えじき, 犠牲, 食いもの bird of prey 猛禽類
- **pride** 名 誇り, 自慢, 自尊心
- **priest** 名 聖職者, 牧師, 僧侶
- **principle** 名 ①原理, 原則 ②道義, 正道
- **prison** 名 ①刑務所, 監獄 ②監禁
- **prisoner** 名 囚人, 捕虜
- **privately** 副 内密に, 非公式に, 個人的に
- **procure** 動 ～を入手する
- **promise** 熟 keep one's promise 約束を守る
- **proof** 名 証拠, 証明
- **proper** 形 適した, 適切な, 正しい
- **prove** 動 ①証明する ②(～であることが)わかる, (～と)なる
- **provide** 動 供給する, 用意する, (～に)備える
- **prowl** 動 うろつく

A B C D E F G H I J K L M N O **P** Q R S T U V W X Y Z

- □ **public** 名一般の人々, 大衆
- □ **pull out** 引き抜く, 引き出す, 取り出す
- □ **punish** 動罰する
- □ **punishment** 名①罰, 処罰 ②罰を受けること
- □ **pursue** 動①追う, 追求する
- □ **put** 熟 put ~ back on its feet ~ を再建する put ~ into … ~を…に突っ込む put down 下に置く, 下ろす put in ~の中に入れる put on ①~を身につける, 着る ②~を…の上に置く put out (明かり・火を) 消す

Q

- □ **quickly** 副敏速に, 急いで
- □ **quietly** 副①静かに ②平穏に, 控えめに

R

- □ **radiate** 動放射する, 発散する
- □ **ragged** 形ぼろぼろの, ぼろを着た
- □ **railing** 名さく, 手すり, レール
- □ **raise** 動①上げる, 高める ②起こす ③~を育てる
- □ **rarely** 副めったに~しない, まれに, 珍しいほど
- □ **rather** 副①むしろ, かえって ②かなり, いくぶん, やや ③それどころか逆に rather like ~に似ている
- □ **reach for** ~に手を伸ばす, ~を取ろうとする
- □ **reach into** ~に手を突っ込む
- □ **reader** 名読者
- □ **realize** 動理解する, 実現する

- □ **rebel** 名反逆者, 反抗者, 謀反人
- □ **recently** 副近ごろ, 最近
- □ **reception** 名もてなし, 迎え入れ
- □ **recognize** 動認める, 認識 [承認] する
- □ **record** 名記録, 登録, 履歴
- □ **recover** 動①取り戻す, ばん回する ②回復する
- □ **recovery** 名回復, 復旧, 立ち直り
- □ **reflect** 動映る, 反響する, 反射する
- □ **refuse** 動拒絶する, 断る
- □ **regain** 動取り戻す, (~に) 戻る
- □ **regiment** 名連隊
- □ **regret** 名遺憾, 後悔
- □ **reinforcement** 名補強, 強化
- □ **release** 動解き放す, 釈放する 名解放, 釈放
- □ **relief** 名 (苦痛・心配などの) 除去, 軽減, 安心
- □ **relieve** 動 (心配・苦痛などを) 軽減する, ほっとさせる
- □ **remain** 動①残っている, 残る ②(~の) ままである [いる]
- □ **rent** 動賃借りする 名使用料, 賃貸料
- □ **repaid** 動 repay (払い戻す) の過去, 過去分詞
- □ **repay** 動①払い戻す, 返金する ②報いる, 恩返しする
- □ **repayment** 名払い戻し, 返済
- □ **repent** 動悔やむ, 後悔する
- □ **reply** 動答える, 返事をする, 応答する 名答え, 返事, 応答
- □ **republic** 名共和国
- □ **request** 名願い, 要求 (物), 需要
- □ **require** 動必要とする, 要する

A
B
C
D
E
F
G
H
I
J
K
L
M
N
O
P
Q
R
S
T
U
V
W
X
Y
Z

☐ **reread** 動再読する, 読み返す

☐ **research** 動調査する, 研究する

☐ **residence** 名住宅, 居住

☐ **resolve** 動決心, 決意

☐ **resourceful** 形機知に富んだ

☐ **respect** 動尊敬[尊重]する

☐ **responsible** 形責任のある, 信頼できる, 確実な

☐ **restoration** 名《the –》王政復古

☐ **reveal** 動明らかにする, 暴露する, もらす

☐ **revolution** 名革命

☐ **revolutionary** 形革命の, 革命的な 名革命家

☐ **revolutionism** 名革命論

☐ **revolutionize** 動大変革[革命]をもたらす

☐ **reward** 名報酬, 償い, 応報

☐ **rhythmic** 形リズミカルな

☐ **right away** すぐに

☐ **right now** 今すぐに, たった今

☐ **rightfully** 副正当に

☐ **rip** 動引き裂く, 切り裂く, 破る

☐ **rob** 動奪う, 金品を盗む, 襲う rob ～ of … ～から…を奪う

☐ **robber** 名泥棒, 強盗

☐ **role** 名①(劇などの)役 ②役割, 任務 take on the role of ～の役割を引き受ける

☐ **roll** 動転がる, 転がす roll down 転がり落ちる

☐ **roof** 名屋根

☐ **rope** 名綱, なわ, ロープ

☐ **rough-looking** 形険しい顔つきの

☐ **roughly** 副手荒く, 粗雑に

☐ **royalism** 名王政主義

☐ **royalist** 名王政主義者

☐ **rubble** 名がれき

☐ **Rue** 名通り, 道《フランス語》

☐ **Rue de Babylone** バビロン通り

☐ **Rue de l'Homme Armé** ロマルメ通り

☐ **Rue de la Chanvrerie** ル・シャヴルリー通り

☐ **Rue de la Verrierie** ヴェルリー通り

☐ **Rue des Filles du Calvaire** フィーユ・ドゥ・カルヴェール通り

☐ **Rue Plumet** プリュメ通り

☐ **ruling** 名裁定, 決定

☐ **rumor** 名うわさ

☐ **run at** ～に向かって走る

☐ **run into** (思いがけず) ～に出会う, ～に駆け込む, ～の中に走って入る

☐ **run off into** ～の中に逃げ込む

☐ **run up** ～に走り寄る

☐ **rush** 動突進する, せき立てる rush into ～に突入する, ～に駆けつける, ～に駆け込む rush out of 急いで～から出てくる

S

☐ **sacrifice** 動 (～に) 生け贄をささげる, (～のために) 犠牲になる

☐ **sadden** 動 (～を) 悲しませる

☐ **sadly** 副悲しそうに, 不幸にも

☐ **saint** 名聖人, 聖徒

☐ **sake** 名 (～の) ため, 利益, 目的

☐ **same ～ as …** 熟《a –》…と同じ(ような) ～

☐ **sank** 動 sink (沈む) の過去

□ **satisfied** 形 満足した be satisfied with ～に満足する

□ **savings** 名 貯金

□ **say to oneself** ひとり言を言う, 心に思う

□ **scale** 動 よじ登る

□ **scar** 名 傷跡

□ **schoolgirl** 名 女子生徒

□ **search** 動 捜し求める, 調べる

□ **secret** 形 秘密の, 隠れた 名 秘密, 神秘

□ **see** 熟 you see あのね, いいですか

□ **seem** 動 (～に) 見える, (～のように) 思われる seem to be ～であるように思われる

□ **Seine (River)** 名 セーヌ川

□ **sentence** 名 判決, 刑罰 動 判決を下す

□ **separate** 動 ①分ける, 分かれる, 隔てる ②別れる, 別れさせる

□ **servant** 名 ①召使, 使用人 ②公務員, (公共事業の) 従業員 civil servant 公務員

□ **serve** 動 ①仕える, 奉仕する ②(役目を) 果たす, 務める, 役に立つ

□ **service** 名 ①勤務, 業務 ②奉仕, 貢献

□ **set up** 配置する, セットする, 据え付ける, 設置する

□ **settle** 動 安定する [させる], 落ち着く, 落ち着かせる

□ **severe** 形 厳しい, 深刻な, 激しい

□ **sewer** 名 下水道

□ **shabby** 形 みすぼらしい, 粗末な, 貧相な, 卑しい

□ **shack** 名 掘っ立て小屋

□ **shade** 名 陰, 日陰

□ **shadow** 名 影

□ **shake** 動 ①振る, 揺れる, 揺さぶる, 震える ②動揺させる

□ **shame** 名 ①恥, 恥辱 ②恥ずべきこと, ひどいこと

□ **shape** 動 形づくる, 具体化する

□ **shatter** 動 打ち砕く, こなごなになる

□ **shed** 動 捨てる, 脱皮する

□ **sheet** 名 (紙などの) 1枚

□ **shelter** 名 ①避難所, 隠れ家 ②保護, 避難

□ **Shhh!** 間 シーッ, しゃべるな

□ **shift** 動 移す, 変える

□ **shiver** 動 (寒さなどで) 身震いする, 震える

□ **shocked** 形 ～にショックを受けて, 憤慨して

□ **shook** 動 shake (振る) の過去

□ **shopping** 名 買い物 go shopping 買い物に行く

□ **shoulder** 名 肩

□ **shrub** 名 低木, 潅木

□ **shudder** 動 身震いする, 震える

□ **shut** 動 ①閉まる, 閉める, 閉じる ②たたむ ③閉じ込める ④shutの過去, 過去分詞

□ **shutter** 名 シャッター, 雨戸

□ **sick in bed** 《be –》病気で寝ている

□ **side** 名 側, 横, そば, 斜面

□ **signature** 名 書名, サイン

□ **significant** 形 ①重要な, 有意義な ②大幅な, 著しい

□ **silence** 名 沈黙, 無言, 静寂 in silence 黙って, 沈黙のうちに

- [ ] **silent** 形 ①無言の, 黙っている ②静かな, 音を立てない
- [ ] **silently** 副 静かに, 黙って
- [ ] **silly** 形 おろかな, 思慮のない
- [ ] **silver** 名 銀, 銀貨, 銀色 形 銀製の
- [ ] **simply** 副 ①簡単に ②単に, ただ ③まったく, 完全に
- [ ] **since** 熟 ever since それ以来ずっと
- [ ] **single** 形 たった1つの
- [ ] **sink** 動 沈む, 沈める, 落ち込む
- [ ] **sit on** ～の上に乗る, ～の上に乗って動けないようにする
- [ ] **sit still** じっとしている, じっと座っている
- [ ] **situation** 名 ①場所, 位置 ②状況, 境遇, 立場
- [ ] **skinny** 形 骨と皮ばかりの, やせた
- [ ] **slam** 動 ばたんと閉める
- [ ] **slave** 名 奴隷 galley slave ガレー船を漕ぐ奴隷
- [ ] **sleeve** 名 袖, たもと, スリーブ
- [ ] **slime** 名 ヘドロ, ドロドロしたもの
- [ ] **slip** 動 滑る, 滑らせる slip out (人が場所から) そっと抜け出す
- [ ] **slowly** 副 遅く, ゆっくり
- [ ] **sly** 形 ずる賢い
- [ ] **smiling** 形 微笑する, にこにこした
- [ ] **so** 熟 and so そこで, それだから, それで or so ～かそこらで so ～ that … 非常に～なので… so many 非常に多くの so that ～するために, それで, ～できるように
- [ ] **soldier** 名 兵士
- [ ] **some** 熟 for some time しばらくの間
- [ ] **somebody** 代 誰か, ある人
- [ ] **somehow** 副 ①どうにかこうにか, ともかく, 何とかして ②どういうわけか
- [ ] **something** 代 ①ある物, 何か ②いくぶん, 多少
- [ ] **sometime** 副 いつか, そのうち
- [ ] **somewhere** 副 ①どこかへ [に] ②いつか, およそ
- [ ] **soon** 熟 as soon as ～するとすぐ, ～するや否や
- [ ] **soul** 名 ①魂 ②精神, 心
- [ ] **spine** 名 背骨, 脊柱
- [ ] **splash** 名 ざぶんという音
- [ ] **spot** 名 地点, 場所
- [ ] **sprang** 動 spring (跳ねる) の過去
- [ ] **spring** 動 飛び出す, 飛びかかる
- [ ] **spy** 名 スパイ
- [ ] **squeeze** 動 絞る, 強く握る, 締めつける
- [ ] **stair** 名 《-s》階段, はしご
- [ ] **stamp** 動 印を押す
- [ ] **stare** 動 じっと [じろじろ] 見る
- [ ] **startle** 動 びっくりさせる, 飛び上がらせる
- [ ] **startled** 形 驚いた, びっくりして
- [ ] **statement** 名 声明, 述べること
- [ ] **stay away** 離れている, 留守にする
- [ ] **steal** 動 盗む
- [ ] **step out of** ～から出る
- [ ] **stern** 形 厳格な, 厳しい
- [ ] **stiff** 形 ①堅い, 頑固な ②堅苦しい
- [ ] **stiffly** 副 硬く, 堅苦しく, ぎこちなく
- [ ] **still** 熟 sit still じっとしている, じっと座っている
- [ ] **stir** 名 動き, かき回すこと

□ **stocking** 名ストッキング, 長靴下

□ **stole** 動 steal (盗む) の過去

□ **stolen** 動 steal (盗む) の過去分詞

□ **stone** 名石, 小石

□ **stoop** 動かがむ

□ **straighten** 動まっすぐにする[なる]

□ **strain** 動緊張させる, ぴんと張る

□ **strangely** 副奇妙に, 変に, 不思議なことに, 不慣れに

□ **stranger** 名①見知らぬ人, 他人 ②不案内[不慣れ]な人

□ **strength** 名①力, 体力 ②長所, 強み ③強度, 濃度

□ **stretch** 動引き伸ばす, 広がる, 広げる stretch out 手足を伸ばす

□ **stride** 動 (急いで) 大股で歩く

□ **striking** 形著しい, 目立つ

□ **strip** 名 (細長い) 1片

□ **strive** 動努力する, 骨を折る

□ **strode** 動 stride (大またで歩く) の過去

□ **stroke** 動なでる, さする

□ **stroll** 動ぶらぶら歩く, 散歩する

□ **strove** 動 strive (努める) の過去

□ **struck** 動 strike (打つ) の過去, 過去分詞

□ **stuff** 動 (~に) 詰め込む

□ **sublimely** 副抜群に

□ **suburb** 名近郊, 郊外

□ **successful** 形成功した, うまくいった

□ **such a** そのような

□ **such as** たとえば~, ~のような

□ **suffer** 動 (病気に) なる, 苦しむ, 悩む

□ **suicide** 名自殺

□ **suit** 名スーツ, 背広

□ **sunset** 名日没, 夕焼け

□ **Superior** 名修道院長 Mother Superior 女子修道院長

□ **supper** 名夕食, 晩さん, 夕飯

□ **support** 動①支える, 支持する ②養う, 援助する 名①支え, 支持 ②援助, 扶養

□ **suppose** 動仮定する, 推測する

□ **surely** 副確かに, きっと

□ **surge** 名 (感情などの) 高まり

□ **surprise** 熟 to one's surprise ~が驚いたことに

□ **surprised** 形驚いた

□ **survive** 動生き残る, 存続する, 切り抜ける

□ **suspect** 動疑う, (~ではないかと) 思う

□ **suspicion** 名容疑, 疑い

□ **suspicious** 形あやしい, 疑い深い

□ **sweat** 動汗をかく

□ **sword** 名①剣, 刀 ②武力

T

□ **take** 熟 take ~ to … ~を…に連れて行く take a bath 風呂に入る take a walk 散歩をする take away ①連れ去る ②取り上げる, 奪い去る ③取り除く take care of ~の世話をする, ~の面倒を見る, ~を管理する take good care of ~を大事に扱う, 大切にする take into 手につかむ, 中に取り入れる take off (衣服を) 脱ぐ, 取り去る take on 雇う, (仕事などを) 引き受ける take on the role of ~

の役割を引き受ける take out 取り出す，取り外す，連れ出す，持って帰る take someone away（人）を連れ出す take someone home（人）を家まで送る

☐ **taken with**《be ~》~に魅了される

☐ **talk of** ~のことを話す

☐ **task** 名（やるべき）仕事，職務

☐ **tell ~ to ...** ~に…するように言う

☐ **tenant** 名 賃借人，住人，テナント

☐ **tenderness** 名 柔らかさ，もろさ，優しさ

☐ **tentatively** 副 ためらいがちに

☐ **testify** 動 証言する，証明する

☐ **thank ~ for** ~に対して礼を言う

☐ **that** 熟 now that 今や~だから，~からには so ~ that … 非常に~なので… so that ~するために，それで，~できるように

☐ **then** 熟 just then そのとたんに

☐ **Thénard** 名 テナール《人名》

☐ **Thénardier** 名 テナルディエ《人名》

☐ **there** 熟 here and there あちこちで there is no way ~する見込みはない there you are その調子，ほら簡単だろう

☐ **these days** このごろ one of these days いずれそのうちに，近日中に

☐ **thief** 名 泥棒，強盗

☐ **thin** 形 薄い，細い，やせた，まばらな

☐ **think of** ~のことを考える，~を思いつく，考え出す

☐ **this** 熟 by this time この時までに，もうすでに in this way このようにして like this このような，こんなふうに

☐ **though** 接 ①~にもかかわらず，~だが ②たとえ~でも

☐ **threaten** 動 脅かす，おびやかす，脅迫する

☐ **through** 熟 come through 通り抜ける get through 乗り切る，~を通り抜ける go through 通り抜ける，一つずつ順番に検討する look through ~をのぞき込む pass through ~を通る，通行する

☐ **throughout** 前 ①~中，~を通じて ②~のいたるところに

☐ **throw away** ~を捨てる；~を無駄に費やす，浪費する

☐ **throw out** 放り出す

☐ **thundering** 形 雷鳴のように響き渡る

☐ **tie up** ひもで縛る，縛り上げる，つなぐ，拘束する

☐ **tightly** 副 きつく，しっかり，堅く

☐ **time** 熟 a hard time つらい時期 all the time ずっと，いつも，その間ずっと by the time ~する時までに by this time この時までに，もうすでに for some time しばらくの間 in time 間に合って，やがて just in time いよいよというときに，すんでのところで，やっと間に合って

☐ **tired** 形 ①疲れた，くたびれた ②あきた，うんざりした be tired of ~に飽きて[うんざりして]いる

☐ **title** 名 肩書，称号

☐ **to one's surprise** ~が驚いたことに

☐ **to the point** 要領を得た

☐ **tone** 名 音，音色，調子

☐ **too ~ to ...** …するには~すぎる

□ **top** 熟 on top of ～の上(部)に

□ **torch** 名 たいまつ, 光明

□ **total** 形 総計の, 全体の, 完全な 名 全体, 合計

□ **Toulons** 名 トゥーロン《地名》

□ **towel** 名 タオル

□ **traditional** 形 伝統的な

□ **tragic** 形 悲劇の, 痛ましい

□ **traitor** 名 反逆者, 裏切り者

□ **transformation** 名 変化, 変換, 変容

□ **traveler** 名 旅行者

□ **treat** 動 扱う

□ **tremble** 動 震える, おののく

□ **trial** 名 裁判

□ **tried** 動 try (試みる)の過去, 過去分詞

□ **triumph** 名 (大)勝利, 大成功, 勝利の喜び

□ **troubled by** 《be –》 ～に悩まされている

□ **truly** 副 ①全く, 本当に, 真に ②心から, 誠実に

□ **truth** 名 ①真理, 事実, 本当 ②誠実, 忠実さ

□ **turn** 熟 turn around 振り向く, 向きを変える, 方向転換する turn away 向こうへ行く, 追い払う, (顔を)そむける, 横を向く turn down 曲がって～へ行く turn into ～に変わる turn to ～の方を向く, ～に頼る, ～に変わる turn white 青ざめる, 血の気が引く

□ **twilight** 名 夕暮れ, 薄明かり

□ **twisted** 形 ねじれた

U

□ **ugly** 形 醜い

□ **Ultimus Fauchelvent** ユルティーム・フォーシュルヴァン《人名》

□ **unable to** 《be –》 ～することができない

□ **uncomfortable** 形 心地よくない

□ **unconscious** 形 無意識の, 気絶した

□ **under arrest** 逮捕されて

□ **unless** 接 もし～でなければ, ～しなければ

□ **unnoticed** 形 気づかれない, 注目されない

□ **unrivaled** 形 匹敵するものがない, 無双の

□ **untie** 動 ほどく

□ **unwrap** 動 包装を解く, 包みを開ける

□ **up to** 熟 ①～まで, ～に至るまで, ～に匹敵して ②《be –》 ～する力がある, ～しようとしている, ～の責任[義務]である

□ **upon** 前 ①《場所・接触》 ～(の上)に ②《日・時》 ～に ③《関係・従事》 ～に関して, ～について, ～して

□ **upper** 形 上の, 上位の, 北方の

□ **upset** 動 気を悪くさせる, (心・神経など)をかき乱す

□ **used to** 動 よく～したものだ, 以前は～であった

□ **usual** 形 通常の, いつもの, 平常の, 普通の as usual いつものように, 相変わらず

□ **utterly** 副 まったく, 完全に

V

- [ ] **various** 形 変化に富んだ, さまざまの, たくさんの
- [ ] **Vernon** 名 ヴェルノン《地名》
- [ ] **very well** 結構, よろしい
- [ ] **vigil** 名 寝ずの番, 徹夜の看病
- [ ] **visit** 熟 pay a visit ～を訪問する
- [ ] **volunteer** 動 自発的に申し出る

W

- [ ] **waist** 名 ウエスト, 腰のくびれ
- [ ] **wait for** ～を待つ
- [ ] **walk** 熟 go for a walk 散歩に行く take a walk 散歩をする walk away 立ち去る, 遠ざかる walk by 通りかかる walk off 立ち去る walk out of ～から出る walk past 通り過ぎる
- [ ] **walled** 形 壁のある, 城壁をめぐらした
- [ ] **wander** 動 ①さまよう, 放浪する, 横道へそれる ②放心する
- [ ] **wandering** 名 放浪
- [ ] **wanted** 形 指名手配の
- [ ] **warn** 動 警告する, 用心させる
- [ ] **watch over** 見守る, 見張る
- [ ] **Waterloo** 名 ワーテルロー《地名。1815年ナポレオン率いるフランス軍が, 英蘭連合軍およびプロイセン軍と戦い敗れた地》
- [ ] **wave** 名 波
- [ ] **way** 熟 all the way ずっと, はるばる, いろいろと along the way 途中で, これまでに in a way ある意味では in this way このようにして lead the way 先に立って導く, 案内する, 率先する make one's way 進む, 行く one's way to (～への) 途中で there is no way ～する見込みはない way of ～する方法 way out 出口, 逃げ道, 脱出方法, 解決法 way to ～する方法

- [ ] **weakly** 副 弱々しく
- [ ] **wealthy** 形 裕福な, 金持ちの
- [ ] **weapon** 名 武器, 兵器
- [ ] **wedding** 名 結婚式, 婚礼
- [ ] **weep** 動 しくしく泣く, 嘆き悲しむ
- [ ] **weigh** 動 圧迫する, 重荷である weigh on ～に重くのしかかる
- [ ] **well** 熟 as well なお, その上, 同様に very well 結構, よろしい
- [ ] **wept** 動 weep (しくしく泣く) の過去, 過去分詞
- [ ] **wheel** 名 輪, 車輪
- [ ] **whenever** 接 ①～するときはいつでも, ～するたびに ②いつ～しても
- [ ] **where to** どこで～すべきか
- [ ] **whether** 接 ～かどうか, ～かまたは…, ～であろうとなかろうと
- [ ] **which** 熟 of which ～の中で
- [ ] **while** 熟 for a while しばらくの間, 少しの間
- [ ] **whisper** 名 ささやき say in a whisper ささやくように言う
- [ ] **white** 熟 turn white 青ざめる, 血の気が引く
- [ ] **whole** 形 全体の, すべての, 完全な, 満～, 丸～ 名 《the –》全体, 全部
- [ ] **whom** 代 ①誰を [に] ②《関係代名詞》～するところの人, そしてその人を
- [ ] **wide** 副 広く, 大きく開いて
- [ ] **widow** 名 未亡人, やもめ
- [ ] **wildly** 副 荒々しく, 乱暴に, むやみに

□ **Will you ~?** ～してくれませんか。

□ **willingly** 副喜んで, 快く

□ **willingness** 名意欲, 快く～すること

□ **wine** 名ワイン, ぶどう酒

□ **wine-shop** 名ワイン専門店

□ **withdrawn** 動 withdraw (引き出す) の過去分詞

□ **withdrew** 動 withdraw (引き出す) の過去

□ **witness** 動目撃する

□ **woke** 動 wake (目が覚める) の過去

□ **womanly** 形女性らしい

□ **wonder** 動①不思議に思う, (～に) 驚く ②(～かしらと) 思う wonder if ～ではないかと思う wonder out loud 疑い [疑問] を口に出す

□ **working** 形働く

□ **world** 熟 in the world 世界で

□ **worry about** ～のことを心配する

□ **worse** 形いっそう悪い, より劣った, よりひどい

□ **worth** 名価値, 値打ち

□ **worthy** 形価値のある, 立派な

□ **Would you like ~?** ～はいかがですか。

□ **would like to** ～したいと思う

□ **wound** 名傷 動負傷させる

□ **wounded** 形負傷した

□ **wretched** 形哀れな, 困った, みじめな, ひどい

□ **wretched-looking** 形惨めな顔つきの

Y

□ **yell** 動大声をあげる, わめく

□ **yet** 熟 and yet それなのに, それにもかかわらず

□ **yew** 名イチイ《植物》

□ **you see** あのね, いいですか

□ **youth** 名若さ, 元気, 若者

やさしい英語を聴いて読む
IBCオーディオブックス

レ・ミゼラブル
Les Misérables
［新装版］

2021年10月4日　第1刷発行

原著者 …… **ヴィクトル・ユーゴー**

リライト …… **ニーナ・ウェグナー**

発行者 …… **浦晋亮**

発行所 …… **IBCパブリッシング株式会社**

　　　　　〒162-0804
　　　　　東京都新宿区中里町29番3号
　　　　　菱秀神楽坂ビル9F
　　　　　Tel. 03-3513-4511
　　　　　Fax. 03-3513-4512
　　　　　www.ibcpub.co.jp

印刷所 …… **株式会社シナノパブリッシングプレス**

CDプレス …… **株式会社ケーエヌコーポレーションジャパン**